9/10   £1.75.

B-25
MITCHELL
at war

Blood-dripping sharkmouth on
B-25C-25 42-64758 retro-
fitted with a G-type nose
packing two .50-cal machine
guns and a 75mm cannon plus
a camera. In olive drab and
white sea search camouflage,
this aircraft was widely
photographed during air to
ground firing tests at the AAF
Tactical Centre, Orlando Field,
Florida, in 1943.
Smithsonian Institution

B-25C-NA 41-12867 was part
of the first model production
batch and aside from the
B-25Bs used on the Doolittle
raid, was the version that
along with the externally
identical D model, introduced
the Mitchell to combat in all
war theatres.
*North American Aviation
(NAA)*

B

B-25 MITCHELL
at war

Jerry Scutts

LONDON

IAN ALLAN LTD

First published 1983

ISBN 0 7110 1219 9

Design: Colin Botwright

© Jerry Scutts 1983

United States distribution by

Motorbooks International
Publishers & Wholesalers Inc
Osceola, Wisconsin 54020, USA ®

Published by Ian Allan Ltd, Shepperton, Surrey
and printed by Ian Allan Printing Ltd at their
works at Coombelands in Runnymede,
England

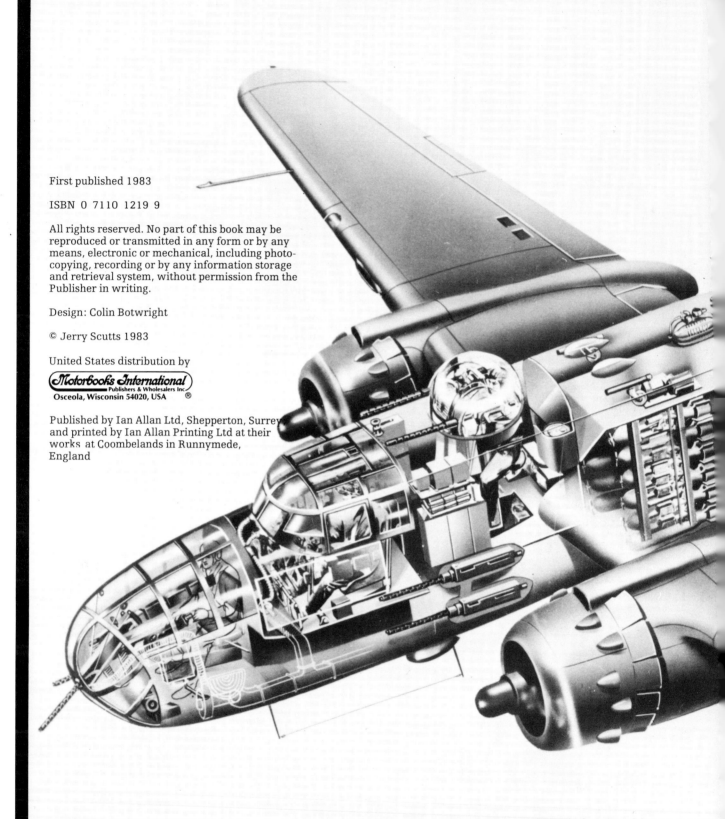

Schematic drawing of the
main equipment, armament
and crew locations in the
B-25J.

Contents

Introduction

Few warplanes of the Second World War saw such widespread service as the North American B-25. Operated with equal success from Europe to China and from the Mediterranean to the Pacific, it emerged as one of the most famous aircraft of that conflict, numerically the most important medium bomber in the US inventory. A large slice of that fame stemmed from the Doolittle raid of April 1942 — indeed it has been said that if the Mitchell had never flown another operation, it would have been remembered for that one. Unequalled in its daring execution and led by one of America'a most accomplished pilots, the Doolittle attack on Japan caught the imagination of the world and even today, the briefest of B-25 references will usually squeeze in a mention of it.

But the full story of the Mitchell is very big indeed. Not only did the aircraft carry out thousands of medium altitude bomb hauls; it patrolled countless tracts of ocean looking for submarines and ships, its weary crews often seeing nothing for hours on end, if at all; it was a transport, flying classroom and test vehicle. And in the Pacific it was the B-25, along with the Douglas A-20, that proved a totally new concept in the deployment of medium and attack bombers. Large enough to carry the machine guns, cannon, bombs and rockets with which to pulverise most targets, the Mitchell came to excel at the hazardous business of low level attack.

While it might be a misnomer to link 'glamour' with any facet of war, low level attack may seem to have more of it — certainly more than medium bombing. In that role the B-25 did not, from some viewpoints, possess the qualities of the Mosquito, which was not really in its class, or the B-26 Marauder, which was. Rather, the B-25 was a solid, dependable aircraft that could be flown competently by pilots without thousands of hours behind them, the men of the 'citizen air forces' demanded by the greatest conflict in history.

Some of those individual experiences are recounted here, but such was the spread of Mitchell squadrons around the globe that no one book could contain all the stories. Instead this one is a number of bites, hopefully juicy enough for most tastes, of a very large apple. I would like to extend a general 'thank you' to all those who replied to my requests for information and dug into their memories and log books to provide some highlights of an unforgettable experience.

Space limitations have meant that accounts of some of the Mitchell's other wartime exploits, including those of the US Marines' PBJ squadrons, have had to be omitted.

Acknowledgements

In preparing an 'at War' title, an author relies on a great number of people to supply information and in this instance, it was particularly gratifying to have the support of the Mitchell's manufacturer. Gene Boswell of the Public Relations side of the North American Aircraft Division of Rockwell International spent a good deal of time making this project a success in the photographic area — as a glance through the following pages will show. Gene has since retired from NAA and I'd like to take this opportunity to wish him well in the future. Special thanks are also due to Bruce Hoy of the National Museum and Art Gallery at Boroko, Papua New Guinea. Bruce has for many years been researching the history of aviation in the southwest Pacific area, a by no means easy task due to the loss or non-existence of records, but he took the time to write helpful letters and supply many photographs.

As always, Frank Smith in Australia responded very quickly to my pleas for photographs, and Howard Levy passed on many pictures of the 12th Bomb Group's activities. Records of the B-25 period of the 319th BG came via Esther and Harold Oyster, whose joint enthusiasm for and knowledge of the group's history is an inspiration to any historian. To them, and all the contributors named herein, thanks indeed.

Equally helpful were the Navy, Marines and Air Force archives of the USA, individual employees of which took the trouble to dig up the material I wanted. Sitting, as it were, in the 'wrong' country, it would be difficult indeed not to have the assistance of these agencies. And last but not least, a special mention for the often maligned postal services of Britain and the USA — without them, much of the foregoing time and effort would have been wasted. To my knowledge, everything arrived safe and sound.

The following people and departments did much of the work: Al Ahlbrecht;

Home is the Hunter: Its well trained gunners still alert for enemy aircraft, an RAF Mitchell II returns to base after a post D-day sortie. Even though the 'infantry' Mitchell crews of 2 Group allowed themselves envious glances at the Mosquito 'cavalry', they did an outstanding job.   *IWM*

Loosing Off: Seven of the nine forward firing guns of a B-25J making impressive flame and smoke during a ground test. *NAA*

Herman Arens; Jim Beavers; Al Behrens; Dana Bell; Sir Leslie Bower; Eugene Boyers of the 14th AF Association; Frederik ter Braak; Gerard Casius; Paul Coggan; Danny Crawford, History and Museums Divn, US Navy; Roger Deckrow; R. E. Casteel; E. J. Dijkstra, Executive Officer of 320 Sqdn, RNLN; H. G. Fitzpatrick; Wallace Forman; A. H. Gilbertson; Bill Goodrich; N. Geldorf; Elaine C. Everly, Military Archives Divn, USN; Charles Hair; Terry Heffernan, A&AEE, Boscombe Down; Stuart Howe; Tom Jones; Hans van der Kop; R. A. Knobloch; Chick Lemley; F. Warren Lovell; Hal Lynch; Ernie McDowell; Ron Mackay; Harry Mangan; Stanley Muniz; Eric Munday; C. E. Myers, Jr; Eugene Olsen; Michael O'Connor; F. C. van Oosten, Commander, R.Neth Navy Dept of History; Lou Peeters; Robert Pettingell; Frank Pine, Tallmantz Aviation; Richard Riding, Editor, *Aeroplane Monthly*; Bruce Robertson; Robert Sarofeen; Malcolm Scott; Chris Shores; Jay Spenser, Smithsonian Institution; Bill Stone; Thomas Thompson; Gordon Swanborough; John Sutay, 57th BW Historian; Victor Tetherington; Norm Taylor; Johan Visser; Dick Ward; Roy Woods; E. R. Wright and Constantine Zakhartchencko. Published information was perused and copied courtesy of the libraries of the UK Civil Aviation Authority and Ministry of Defence and among the UK photographic sources were the Imperial War Museum, the staff of which were extremely helpful at all times. Many American contributions came via letters published in magazines such as *Naval Aviation News* and *Air Classics*, and an appreciation of their space is extended to their editors.

Jerry Scutts

Baker Two Five

In the mid-1930s, the US Army Air Corps began seriously to consider replacing the aircraft then in use by its ground support or 'attack' squadrons. Traditionally, all previous types in this category had been powered by a single engine but, influenced by reports of the light, twin-engined bombers being developed in Europe, the Army invited industry to design similar aircraft. A circular proposal was issued for a design competition for twin-engined attack bombers capable of carrying a 1,200lb bomb load a distance of 1,200 miles at a speed of 200mph. These minimum requirements were met by four companies which submitted proposals in July 1938. Bell offered the Model 9, Stearman the X-100, Martin the 167F and Douglas entered with the Model 7B.

These companies were asked to build prototypes and offer them for evaluation by 17 March 1939, by which time Bell, the only concern to tender a design powered by in-line engines, had dropped out to be replaced by North American Aviation with the NA-40. Thus Martin, NAA, Douglas and to a lesser extent Stearman, established design parameters for all American twin-engined bombers of the World War 2 period. All the prototypes had a number of common features, including radial engines driving three-bladed propellers and retractable undercarriages. Each aircraft also accommodated bombs in an internal fuselage bay and defensive armament consisted of .30-cal machine guns. A high wing arrangement was shared by the Stearman and North American designs, the latter and the Douglas Model 7B also employing a tricycle landing gear.

Although it is considered the progenitor of the B-25, the NA-40 was merely an experimental bridge between the Mitchell and the XB-21 of 1937, NAA's only previous twin-engined type. An attempt to improve on the performance of the Douglas B-18 which it resembled, the XB-21 failed to win an Air Corps order and only one example was built. The NA-40 was an entirely different machine: a high wing monoplane with a deep, slab-sided fuselage, it had twin fins and rudders and extensive nose glazing over the bombardier's position. The pilot and co-pilot were seated in tandem under an elongated 'greenhouse' canopy similar to that fitted to many NAA trainer aircraft. A radioman/gunner occupied a mid-fuselage station, the fifth man acting mainly as a gunner. Defensive armament consisted of seven .30-cal machine guns; the bombardier had a single gun firing through a rotating blister set on top of the nose cone, a second was mounted in a dorsal blister aft of the wing and a third could be fired through a tunnel in the fuselage floor. Four guns were fixed in the leading edges of the wing, outboard of the engines.

The powerplants originally fitted were Pratt & Whitney R-1830-S6C3-G 14-cylinder Twin Wasp radials, each rated at 1,100hp and positioned in nacelles which terminated in a squared-off section just aft of the wing trailing edge. The wing

1
Getting down to some of the paperwork circa 1941 are 'Dutch' Kindelberger (left) and 'Lee' Atwood, two of the men primarily responsible for the B-25. *NAA*

1

2
Test Pilots: Joe Barton (left) and Ed Virgin took up six of the B-25 production and experimental prototypes on · their maiden flights. Barton flew the XB-25E (42-32281) a C model fitted with hot-air leading edge de-icing, the NA-98X (43-4406) with 2,000hp R-2800s in elongated cowlings, and the B-25J, Virgin the B-25A, B-25C and XB-25G (41-13296) the first cannon armed Mitchell. *NAA*

itself was of 66ft span and had constant root to tip dihedral. Gross weight of the NA-40 was 19,500lb.

The NA-40 was built at Inglewood, California, then North American's only manufacturing plant, situated on the northwest corner of Imperial Highway and Aviation Boulevard on the site now occupied by Los Angeles international airport. Roll-out took place in January 1939 and on 10 February, the NA-40 flew for the first time in the hands of engineering test pilot Paul Balfour. Allocated the AAC serial number 40-1052, but otherwise known as the X14221, the NA-40 revealed a promising performance, although its top speed was a little below expectations, at 265mph. Consequently, the engines were changed before the end of February, to 1,350hp Wright GR-2600-A71s — not only

more powerful, but physically larger — in which form the aircraft became the NA-40B or NA-40-2 in NAA nomenclature.

With preliminary company flight testing completed, the NA-40 was flown from Inglewood to Wright Field, Ohio, to take part in the Air Corps' attack bomber evaluation and competition. Although gross weight had risen to 21,000lb, speed had been increased to 285mph and initial military trials were encouraging. There followed a two-week period of testing to confirm the aircraft's suitability as an Army attack bomber, during which Major Younger Pitts, assigned to Wright Field to help fill a shortage of test pilots, flew the aircraft. It was during the final phase of one flight that disaster struck; Major Pitts made to enter the Wright Field approach pattern whereupon he apparently lost

3

3
Going Straight: Continuous wing dihedral hall marked the first nine B-25s. Very light on the controls, they were found to be a little too sensitive for accurate bombing and the distinctive gull wing was created to give more positive feel. *NAA*

4
Immediate antecedent to the NA-62 was the NA-40, only the second twin that North American had built. Although in existence only for some three months it was able to provide valuable data on which to base the much-improved Mitchell prototype. The NA-40 is seen here soon after roll-out and before the airframe received a high polish for the official unveiling. *NAA*

control and there was a high speed crash. The resultant fire destroyed the NA-40, although the crew escaped unharmed. A subsequent Wright Field report exonerated any failure of the aircraft as a contributory cause of the accident, which was traced to a newly-designed propeller pitch control.

With the sole NA-40 written off, the Army's attention focused on the Douglas Model 7B, which subsequently became the first of the new attack bombers to be ordered for the US military. Martin's Model 167 was built almost entirely for Allied nations and the Stearman X-100 was purchased by the USAAC as the sole X-21. In the meantime, a new circular proposal for a medium bomber had been promulgated on 25 January 1939, the Air Corps having established a requirement for two aircraft in each bomber category — attack, medium and heavy. Little time was

lost; designs had to be submitted by 5 July and there would be no wait for prototypes to be constructed, as per previous practice. In North American's case there was little need, for the company had comprehensive development plans available for the NA-40 (up to NA-40-7) and these became the basis for a medium bomber project. The unfortunately brief flight test and handling reports on the NA-40 stood the company in good stead to meet the new requirement. Particularly useful was the work done on a tricycle landing gear, which was to become a standard feature of all new US bombers. The NA-40's crew accommodation of five seats was also specified, along with a top speed above 300mph, a range of 2,000 miles and a 3,000lb bomb load.

Data on 83 different design combinations was

4

submitted to the Army by NAA's design office, then headed by John Lee Atwood and Raymond H. Rice. Closing date for proposals was 10 September 1939 and on the 20th, all the hard work over the preceeding few months was rewarded by a $11,771,000 contract for 184 examples of a medium bomber known by the company as the NA-62. The other production Army medium bomber, Martin's B-26, was ordered the same day.

Among the different designs put forward for the NA-62, both single and twin vertical tail surfaces were considered, along with detail variations, including a 'stepped' fuselage coaming with a dorsal gun position similar to that of the A-20, and a very streamlined aircraft that looked very much like a Marauder. In fact, with some 80 variations, North American was able to incorporate most design features of

all US WW2 bombers in some form or another. What finally emerged was not particularly revolutionary, but rather a strong, reliable airframe that would not create too many production problems — and become one of the most successful combat aircraft ever procured by the Army.

Although the NA-62 was a completely different machine, it retained some of the external features of the NA-40, including unbroken wing dihedral and twin fins and rudders, although as it transpired, the first NA-62 had smaller area vertical tail surfaces, which were later changed to units almost identical to those of the NA-40. The most striking difference between the two aircraft was in the fuselage; the NA-62 had a far slimmer fuselage profile than its predecessor, and the engine nacelles were

5
Air Corps crews collecting new B-25s from the factory received the VIP treatment, complete with chauffeur-driven company Pontiac to carry the flight bags. Serial numbers were not applied to the vertical tail surfaces of the early model B-25s, although the last four digits were affixed under the rear gunner's cupola of each aircraft. *NAA*

6
Having flown what is still regarded as the most famous B-25 operation of them all on 18 April 1942, the 17th Bomb Group did not subsequently use Mitchells in combat. Its WW2 service was with Marauders in the MTO and still later came Korea and the A-26 Invader. But in late 1941 the group was still the premier AAF B-25 unit with both straight and gull winged models on strength.
Bowers via Gordon Swanborough

7
Fine view of a B-25 showing the glazed rear fuselage and dorsal gun hatches to advantage. Also visible is the tail end 'stinger', a heavily-framed position designed for a single .50-cal machine gun.
NAA

7

finely tapered. Powerplants were two 1,700hp Wright R-2600-9 Cyclone radials.

The pilot and co-pilot were housed in side-by-side seats under a stepped canopy aft of a glazed bombardier's station in the extreme nose and the crew was made up by two gunners, one acting as flight engineer. One of the gunners adopted a prone position to fire a single machine gun from the extreme tail end of the fuselage — one reason why a twin tail configuration, which cleared the field of fire — was chosen. There was no powered gun position in the NA-62, although additional weapons could be used from two rear fuselage side hatches and a dorsal hatch aft of the wing. Apart from the tail 'stinger', all guns were of the rifle-calibre .30in M-2 type.

Much of the information necessary for NAA engineers to create the NA-62 came from the results of wind tunnel tests with a one-ninth scale model, which was built as soon as the Air Corps accepted the final design. One of the first such models to have electric motors to turn its propellers, this tiny aircraft model was invaluable in calculating weight, performance and stalling characteristics. NAA also made extensive use of the Pasadena facilities of the California Institute of Technology, the effort required to design the full size aircraft eventually totalling over 156,000 engineering manhours and the preparation of 8,500 original drawings.

Concurrent with construction of the wind tunnel model, work started on a full scale wooden mock-up, which was to be

complete down to seats, controls and full instrumentation. An Army mock-up board made an inspection prior to approving the layout on 4 November 1939. The war in Europe was two months old, almost to the day.

In common with other US aviation companies, North American faced a number of problems in meeting unprecedentally high production orders for combat aircraft. Primarily, these were space, manpower and materials; by the end of 1939, NAA had a backlog of orders worth £50million and the Inglewood plant area had outgrown even the 418,000sq ft it had expanded to at the start of 1939. An additional 236,000sq ft of production space was under construction, yet more would soon be needed, particularly for an aircraft the size of the B-25. Building thousands of twin-engined bombers was the largest project the firm had ever undertaken. Therefore, plans were made to open a new plant specifically for this purpose, in Kansas City. In the event, this facility turned out 6,680 of the total 9,816 B-25s built, the balance coming off the Inglewood line.

Lack of personnel led the company to introduce a long list of employee benefits to forestall losing its skilled people to other sectors of industry and the armed forces. Widespread enthusiasm for the 'big new bomber' helped a great deal in this respect, NAA workers widely regarding the B-25 as the most prestigious project the company handled during the war. This attitude was due mainly to the size of the aircraft, for a workforce used to making single-engined trainers saw 'their' bomber as a powerful means of hitting back at the enemy — far more so than a fighter, even one of the calibre of the P-51.

The Kansas City plant was all but complete the day the Japanese attacked Pearl Harbor and for the duration of the war, was operated under the Knudsen Plan, which called for the automobile industry to switch to the manufacture of aircraft sub-assemblies for 'the duration'. Under the plan, the established aviation manufacturers managed the plants and directed final assembly. In North American's case, the supplier was General Motors' Fisher Body Division. Day to day plant operation was similar to that at both Inglewood and Dallas (the second NAA plant, opened in March 1941) except that Kansas was a government-built factory, on whose behalf NAA ran it.

By 4 July 1940, an NA-62 static test airframe had been sent to Wright Field while work proceeded on the first production airframe, 40-2165. It was completed in August and on the 19th, Vance Breeze undertook the maiden flight, accompanied by test engineer Roy Ferren. Resplendent in gleaming aluminium finish and Air Corps markings, the first-ever B-25 performed well, better in fact than its designers had predicted. In particular, top speed was higher than estimated, although landing speed was felt to be low enough for an aircraft of the size to be flown from unprepared airstrips, an asset which was to prove invaluable.

Wright Field found that the NA-62 suffered some loss of directional stability, due mainly to the excessive wing dihedral and the aircraft also had a tendency to Dutch roll, making it difficult to fly straight and level. It was recommended that the wing sections outboard of the engine nacelles be brought down to the absolute horizontal, leaving the dihedral inboard. This cured the instability problem and the cranked or

8
A slight drawback of the B-25 was a nosewheel unforgiving of rough treatment. The Wright Field report on this 27 September 1941 mishap to the third production aircraft (40-2167) stated that the pilot, Maj H. F. Gregory, failed to notice that the nosewheel had not straightened after he taxied from the parking position and had in fact, rolled into sandy loam. When the wheel hit the edge of a paved surface and the aircraft stopped, the throttles were advanced — whereupon the oleo collapsed. Only pilot pride was injured.
Smithsonian Institution

'gull' wing, incorporated on the tenth production B-25 (40-2174) became one of the major recognition points of the type. Early in production, the B-25 was named 'Mitchell' in honour of the late General William 'Billy' Mitchell, who had done so much to show the need for a force of bombers with the capabilities of the B-25. Prophetically, Mitchell's 1921 bombing trials had shown the effectiveness of aerial bombs against warships, a form of attack in which the aircraft named after him was to excel.

If the early B-25s lacked anything, it was in defensive armament, a drawback in which it was certainly not unique. Without a single machine gun in any form of powered position, the aircraft appeared to enforce current military thinking that a medium bomber had only to use its speed to evade enemy fighters. Notwithstanding reports from Europe, this doctrine was adhered to, with the result that without exception, American bombers went into action chronically ill-armed for the type of war they had to fight. The perchant of Japanese and German fighters for the damaging, often fatal head-on attack was to cost the USAAF dear in the first months of combat.

In one respect, the early B-25 had a slight advantage over its contemporaries — its .50-cal in the tail. Although it became generally agreed that nose, rather than tail defence was what counted in the type of mission the B-25 was to fly in the Pacific, extreme tail guns were installed on the majority of production models. The first B-25 model was therefore, a step in the right direction, although the tail gun was soon deleted and was not replaced on production lines until the advent of the deep rear fuselage models, the B-25H and J, leaving combat units to put back the 'sting in the tail'.

Not that any shortcomings in armament gave cause for concern when the B-25 began to be issued to operational squadrons; the first recipients were eager to fly the new 'hot ship' which was comfortable, fast and easy to handle and an all-round improvement on the B-18 and its ilk, which was standard USAAC equipment in 1940. The first unit to receive the B-25, in late February 1941, was the 17th Bombardment Group (Medium), based at McChord Field in Washington State with its component 34th, 37th and 94th Squadrons, plus the attached 89th Reconnaissance. First B-25 received by the group was the fourth production machine, 40-2168, one of the nine built with the original straight wing, but in other respects similar to all subsequent aircraft. A change

that had already been made on all B-25s irrespective of wing design was the shape of the fin and rudder assembly. Gone were the small 'pyramid' units with which the NA-62 first flew, to be replaced by the tapering, squared-off surfaces similar to those of the NA-40. These had been found to bestow adequate stability, although 40-2165 had been flown with 'square' vertical tail surfaces during its test programme.

As B-25s were delivered to the 17th Group, individual aircraft were assigned to each squadron in order that as many pilots as possible could fly them before enough were on hand to equip the entire group. Thus, the first machine was assigned to Headquarters Squadron, the second (40-2169) to the 34th and so forth. By the summer of 1941, the group was fully equipped with both straight and gull-winged models and working up on the new type. A number of changes of base were made during 1941, taking in Pendleton, Oregon, Lexington County airport, South Carolina and Felts Field, Washington. By the time of Pearl Harbor, the group had flown numerous coastal patrols over the Atlantic and the Gulf of Mexico, on the lookout for enemy submarines. In fact, the frequent change of location had seen the group's B-25s out over much of the coastal waters of the United States on a duty that was to become very familiar to Mitchell crews all over the world in the next few years.

Interspersed with anti-sub patrols were Army manouevres, a great deal of practice flying and 'spit and polish' inspections by high ranking officers. With a mixture of initial production B-25s as well as modified wing models, the 17th Group was uniquely placed to test the difference between the two. Few problems were actually found with the straight wing machines, apart from a tendency to skid off line during bombing runs. The aircraft was stable enough, but it was found that when pilots tried to follow the PDI — Pilot's Directional Indicator — signals from the bombardier by making small corrections with the rudders, a wing would lift. If this happened at the time of bomb release, correction would not prevent the bombs being tossed sideways and causing them to miss the target. The gull wing apparently cured the problem, although there was a small penalty in that the very light 'hands off' characteristics were changed.

'Bugs' of some form or another are common in any new aircraft and the B-25 was no exception. One more serious than that traced to the original wing was rupturing of fuel hoses. During

9
North American's firm grip on international medium bomber requirements made good publicity shots in the early days. All aircraft visible were from the first B-25C production batch and have US, Russian, Dutch and British markings — but records would appear to indicate that only the Russian aircraft was actually delivered to the country in question, the remainder being re-allocated to the USAAF. The man on the fuselage of the nearest machine is about to remove the protective cocoon over the turret. *NAA*

manoeuvres in Carolina in 1941, the 17th Bomb Group had a number of B-25A models blow up just as they became airborne. No apparent cause was found until tests proved that self-sealing compound in the fuel hoses was rupturing on the inside of the hose and swelling it almost closed. Engine run up prior to take off had been normal, as the damaged hoses were letting through just enough fuel for the engines to warm up, but they could not sustain the flow for maximum take off power. All B-25As were grounded until improved hoses were fitted.

Self-sealing fuel tanks and armour plate had been added to the 25th B-25 off the production line to create the B-25A model, otherwise similar to earlier examples. The first flight was made by Edward Virgin on 25 February 1941. Inevitably, this added 'combat-worthiness' increased weight, which had to be paid for: fuel capacity was

reduced by 246gal, range was cut by 750 miles and top speed dropped to 315mph. Service ceiling was also less, at 27,000ft rather than 30,000ft and the aircraft's rate of climb was slightly slower. But the B-25 was already beginning to show the soundness of the basic design by absorbing additional equipment without too much detrimental effect — such was the lot of virtually every good first-line combat aircraft of WW2, few of which, to the credit of their designers, failed to stand being turned into efficient fighting machines. Production of the B-25A ran to 40 before the B-25B emerged, this model marking the first major attempt to increase defensive firepower.

In the course of producing the B-25A, North American was able to study more reports from the European war zone, particularly on light bomber operations. They did not offer much comfort. Rather, they

emphasised the many deficiencies of British, French, German and Italian bombers that had been designed years before the war with their eventual deployment little more than optimistic hypothesis. It was equally clear that if the US intention was to use its bombers, including B-25s, in Europe, they would not fare well against enemy fighters in their under-armed form.

NAA therefore set about beefing up the armament of the B-25 with all speed. Compared to RAF bombers, almost universally armed with guns mounted in powered turrets, the B-25 and other American bombers of the period were poorly defended, their hand-held machine guns lacking both accuracy and destructive power at contemporary air combat speeds. Aerodynamists worked on the problem and decided that the Mitchell airframe could take two power-operated turrets. All guns except the .30-cal weapon in the bombardier's compartment were removed; the perspex hatch for a single dorsal gun was faired over and the rear fuselage side hatches were reduced in size. A Bendix power turret was fitted into the dorsal position, approximately where the gun hatch had been and on the undersides of the fuselage a well was cut to accommodate a

remotely-sighted and fired 'solid' turret approximately in line with the end of the engine nacelles. Also made by Bendix, this latter installation was almost fully retractable, the twin .50-in gun barrels fitting into slots in the fuselage underside when it was in the fully up position. A system of mirrors working on the periscope principle enabled the gunner (often in theory only) to sight and fire the weapons.

Flight tests of the B-25B were made at Wright Field in the spring of 1941 and apart from some expected loss of 'feel' due to the additional weight of the turrets, few adverse effects were reported. The extensive engineering changes necessary to fit the new gun positions were made smoothly and 100 examples were built before the end of 1941, production running to 120 machines.

Again the 17th BG was the first unit to receive a new B-25 model, although the majority were destined to serve as trainers for the steadily-increasing number of new combat crews. Part of their training was to maintain the coastal watch for Axis submarines, the B-25 joining a homogenous collection of second-line bombers tasked to guard the approaches to the continental USA. Reconnaissance groups, among them the 66th and 69th and single squadrons

10
Down the line: Inglewood humming to the sound of B-25 production. The red centre to the national insignia dates the photograph as earlier than August 1942, when the all-white star marking was introduced. Of interest is the fact that the insignia was applied before camouflaging was completed, necessitating masking. *NAA*

such as the 18th, attached to the 22nd Bomb Group, also received new B-25Bs. Subsequent years would see Mitchells equipping many of the bomb groups then forming specifically for combat training, two of the first being the 309th at Davis Monthan Field, Arizona and the 334th at Greenville, SC. These and other units were part of America's five home-based wartime air forces, the 1st, 2nd, 3rd and 4th, tasked with the dual role of training and national defence, and the 6th, assigned to the protection of the Canal Zone.

Training was also the lot of the 23 B models delivered to the RAF under the Lend Lease Bill, signed on 11 March 1941 and leading to the establishment of the Office of Lend-Lease Administration on 28 October. By then Russia was officially included in the nations scheduled to receive war supplies from the US Government. Accordingly, during the Second Soviet Protocol (1 July 1942 to 30 June 1943) deliveries of aircraft began via the northwestern ferry route through Alaska to Siberia — the Alsib programme.

Russian association with the B-25 had begun in the autumn of 1941 when a group of pilots was sent to McChord, home of the 17th BG and, by all accounts, the visitors were well pleased by what they saw. The B-25 became the first US bomber type supplied to the Soviet Union, 862 examples out of 870 despatched arriving at their destination. Five models — B-25B, C, D, G and J served the Red Air Force.

Captain Ted W. Lawson in his graphic *Thirty Seconds Over Tokyo* relates how he met the Russians who visited the 17th and later, experienced one of the most hair-raising flights of his life as a B-25 with a Russian general at the controls, proceeded to beat up Washington. Transition training facilities had been provided for the Russians at nearby Fort George and their initial enthusiasm for the B-25 made it their first choice of the multi-engined aircraft offered by the US.

With suitable airfields established in Canada and Alaska, the American ferry operation gradually gained impetus, even though the Russians did not formally agree the Alsib route until July 1942. In practice, 'agreement' meant little, as the Soviets constantly delayed decisions on bases and ferry routings, particularly when it came to foreign crews overflying their territory, notwithstanding their urgent need for war material at that time.

An initial proposal to have 155 bombers and fighters, of which 12 were B-25s, delivered to Siberia by early August 1942

11
Part of the B-25C-5 batch undergoing final assembly outdoors, work being shared between the mediums and the other priority NAA wartime product, the P-51. *NAA*

was revised when the Russians refused on the grounds that their bases were unable to handle so many aircraft. Consequently on 24 September, Soviet airmen began arriving at Fairbanks, Alaska to collect them. Despite continuing Soviet deviousness, 369 machines had been flown out by March 1943.

It was generally agreed that the Russians were fine pilots, although the Americans winced at their habit of revving up cold engines to full power in sub-zero temperatures, tearing down the runway and hauling off, immediately executing highly dangerous low level turns. There were incidents and accidents and some strained Soviet-American relations, but the flow of aircraft through Alaska was maintained until the end of the war. The fate of most of them is still unrecorded in the West, apart from occasional references in articles and books. The 22nd Division of the Long Range Aviation Service is stated to have used B-25s during the Battle of Stalingrad, when they presumably acquitted themselves well. A glance at the other side of the coin is given by German night fighter ace Wilhelm Johnnen in his book *Duel Under the Stars* wherein he recounts the destruction of three B-25s engaged in partisan supply flights over Hungary in the summer of 1944. Semi-official Soviet war histories tend to overlook the contribution of 14,833 Allied aircraft supplied to aid the 'Great Patriotic War' and cite only the achievements of warplanes built in the state factories.

On 9 November 1941, Ed Virgin flew the first example of the fourth Mitchell production model, NAA charge number NA-83, the B-25C. Ordered by the Army on 28 September 1940, this version and the similar D model were the first of the B-25s to be mass-produced, by the Inglewood and Kansas City plants respectively. Following 863 B-25C-NA and C-1 aircraft were 162 B-25C-5s (NA-90) intended for the Netherlands East Indies, all of which

were transferred to the USAAF, the Dutch instead receiving quantities of C, C-1, D and subsequent models. There followed 145 B-25C-10s (NA-94) for Britain and 149 C-15s (NA-93) for China under Defence Aid; 200 C-20 models and 100 C-25s (both with charge No NA-96).

A number of refinements were incorporated into the early B-25Cs as production proceeded: armament was further increased by a single .50-cal machine gun fixed in the lower starboard side of the bombardier's compartment and fired from the cockpit, the flexible .30 gun for use by the bombardier being replaced by a .50-cal weapon. External wing bomb racks able to accommodate up to 2,500lb were introduced, as were fuselage shackles for a 22.4in torpedo weighing 2,000lb. A Sperry automatic pilot, first used on the Tokyo raid B-25Bs, was installed in both the C and D model during production. The fitting of extra fuel tanks on the Doolittle aircraft pointed the way to similar additional capacity on all subsequent models, bomb bay tankage varying according to range and offensive load considerations. Although the Bendix lower turret was factory-fitted on the majority of aircraft, most operational USAAF machines had this cumbersome item removed, either at modification centres such as that operated by Trans World Airlines at Kansas City, or in the field. The resultant space allowed for the fitting of a 'turret tank' or hand-held machine guns on a swivel mounting in the fuselage floor — or more commonly, twin waist gun windows in each side of the fuselage.

As the NA-87, the first of 200 B-25Ds flew on 3 January 1943, production running to 1,790 in eight sub-types, 171 more than C produciton. The first six sub-types were built under NAA charge No NA-87, the last two under NA-100. Breakdowns were: 200 B-25D; 100 D-1; 225 D-5; 180 D-10; 180 D-15; 315 D-20; 340 D-30 and 250 D-35.

12
Early in September 1942, this B-25B landed at Fairbanks, Alaska to become the first Mitchell passed to the Russians. Ladd Field records state the number of Mitchells ferried through for collection as 732, although other sources quote a slightly higher figure. *USAF*

18

Mitchell Walkround

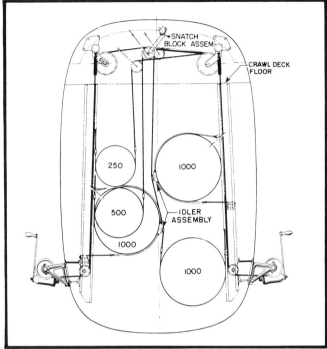

13
The cockpit layout of the early model Mitchells was similar and the multiplicity of levers on the central pedestal was common to the entire series with only detail changes. This view includes controls for elevator trim, propeller speed, mixture, superchargers and cooling gills. *NAA*

14
Diagram showing the various bomb sizes that could be accommodated in the B-25's internal bay, together with the hoist system used. *NAA*

15
Bomb bay detail viewed from the rear of the aircraft with an unfinned bomb 'on the sling'. *NAA*

16
A 2,000-pounder attached to the centre carrier lugs. This size was the largest bomb a B-25 could carry. *NAA*

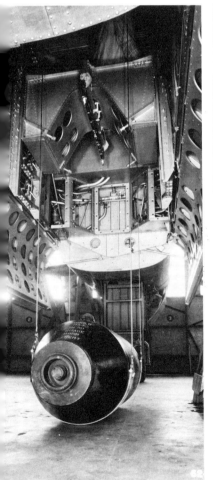

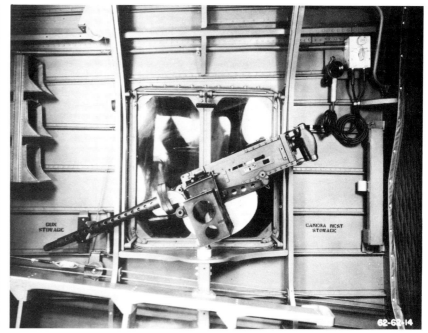

17
Prior to the introduction of a dorsal turret on the B model, the Mitchell's defence rested on hand-held machine guns on single mountings. This was how the dorsal .30-cal weapon was stowed beneath its operating hatch on the top of the fuselage. *NAA*

18
The two-section rear fuselage side windows were a carry-over from the NA-40 and were retained only for a short time before being changed for a single perspex panel on the B-25B. The limited field of fire and need for a larger hatch can be appreciated. The gun is a .30-cal weapon. *NAA*

19

19
A step in the right direction: the Bendix L-type dorsal turret with twin 'fifties, each with 440 rounds, gave the B-25B its first really effective form of defence. There were however, teething troubles with early turret installations and the guns could not sweep large areas directly to the rear and in front of the aircraft. *Smithsonian Institution*

20
Not such a good idea was the crank-down ventral turret. Although aerodynamically better than some of the Heath Robinson devices invented for dorsal defence elsewhere, it was too complex for the rapid tracking and firing that WW2 combat required. Before a single round could leave the barrels, the gunner had to go through 11 operations to lower the turret, charge the guns and sight the target, resting his chest on the pad (shown in the centre of the photograph) and screw his eye into the pad at the top of the column.
Smithsonian Institution

21
It took 55 seconds to get the 600lb turret to its fully lowered, operating position. It was invariably removed from most aircraft exposed to the realities of combat, at least in American hands. Curiously, the RAF Mitchell squadrons persevered with it.
Smithsonian Institution

22
The Bendix turret fully down and theoretically ready to give attacking fighters a hot reception . . . at least it had two nice big 'fifties that could be more effectively mounted elsewhere in the aircraft, and its space could conveniently be used for an extra fuel tank.
Smithsonian Institution

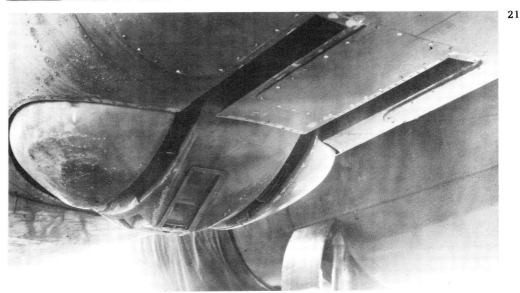

Special Project

When the B-25 made its combat debut in WW2 by bombing Japanese targets in the south-west Pacific on 5 April 1942, the fact was hardly noted in the American press, so bad was the war situation almost everywhere. But 13 days later there was a very big story to tell. Banner headlines proclaimed that US bombers had attacked the very heart of the Japanese empire, nothing short of Tokyo itself. The intrepid leader of the force, James H. Doolittle, became America's first national hero of the war. Pulses raced at some good news at last and questions came thick and fast. People wanted to know how such a raid had been possible and where the bombers had flown from. At a press conference on 21 April, President Roosevelt simply said that they had come from 'Shangri-La'. That allusion to the mythical land described in James Hilton's novel *Paradise Lost* indicated that the true location would have to remain secret for the time being. And although there was informed speculation that the Mitchells had used an aircraft carrier, no-one was really sure until about a year later, when the name of the USS *Hornet* was confirmed.

Difficult to quantify in military terms, for few records of the actual damage were ever found, the Tokyo raid was undoubtedly a long overdue boost to Allied fortunes and a grave warning to the Japanese. If nothing else it was a monumental loss of face to a nation at the very peak of conquest and a considerable influence on future strategy, leading to a strengthening of home defence and giving impetus to the Imperial Navy's greatest disaster at Midway that summer.

When a plan to strike Japan with Army bombers ferried close to the home islands by aircraft carrier was approved in principle, little time was lost in confirming

23
Half the Doolittle force ranged on *Hornet*'s aft flight deck includes B-25B 40-2303, the aircraft assigned to Lt Harold Watson, in the immediate foreground. Lt Richard Joyce's 40-2250 is slotted in behind it. *US Navy*

that it would work in practice. Army pilot John E. Fitzgerald accordingly conducted a series of flight tests with three B-25s at Norfolk NAS, Virginia. The tests culminated in two carrier take offs, Fitzgerald having found that a B-25 loaded to 23,000, 26,000 and 29,000lb could leave the ground safely in less than 800ft. On the morning of 2 February, two aircraft (the third had gone unserviceable) were hoisted aboard the *Hornet*, which had arrived in Norfolk on 31 January to receive orders for her first war assignment.

The carrier sailed that morning and launched both B-25s without difficulty, Fitzgerald having calculated that even loaded to 31,000lb, pilots would experience few problems if there was a good headwind down the deck. He noted that in such conditions, the B-25's ASI had read 45mph even before the aircraft moved, so only an extra 23mph would be necessary to reach the optimum speed of 68mph for a safe take off.

Doolittle meanwhile busied himself with the details of 'Special Aviation Project No 1', which included organising modifications to 24 (18 for the operation, plus six

24
Interesting but unfortunately unidentified nose art on one of the Tokyo raid Mitchells. As was common practice when a Norden was installed, a shroud has also been placed over the 'Mark Twain' sight specially made for the mission. *USN*

25
Under undoubtedly watchful eyes aboard the cruiser *Nashville*, Army pilots run up engines as part of the daily routine during the *Hornet's* run across the Pacific. *USN*

Still perhaps a little sceptical about the whole idea, on watch seamen survey the *Hornet*'s unique 'air group'. In the immediate foreground is Lt Ted Lawson's B-25B 40-2261, with Lt Edward York's 40-2242 behind. As well as a number '3' on its nose — presumably a plane-in-squadron designator — the latter machine appears to have the dark blue cowling rings of the 34th Squadron. *USN*

spares) B-25Bs by Mid-Continent Airlines at its maintenance base at Wold Chamberlain Airport in Minneapolis. Doolittle's requirements included fitting an extra 265gal fuel tank and associated 'plumbing' in the bomb bay roof, with a 175gal flexible bag type tank forward; adding de-icer boots to all flying surface leading edges and positioning shackles for four 500lb bombs. The de-icers were ordered in case the Mitchell's exit route after the attack was north to Vladivostock, where severe weather could be expected.

While Mid-Continent worked on the aircraft, Doolittle deliberated on targets, routes and eventual destinations for his force, keeping Roosevelt informed via Gen Arnold. Landing grounds in Chinese territory were finally chosen and the targets were narrowed down to military and industrial installations in Tokyo-Yokohama, Nagoya and Osaka-Kobe. With

the aircraft launched from the nearest practical point to Japan, each B-25 would carry four 500lb demolition bombs and nearly 1,000lb of incendiaries in clusters of 48 each, the bombs to be dropped first.

Men from the 17th Bomb Group and 89th Reconnaissance Squadron formed the flight crews, the four squadron commanders making the choice. Some mixing of men from different units was necessary in order to have the most experienced individuals in each B-25 that would fly the mission. On 3 February, the 17th Group moved to Columbia AAF, SC, from whence two dozen crews transferred, with their ground echelons, to Eglin, Florida. There they were received by Lt 'Hank' Miller, a Navy instructor from Pensacola who was to train Army crews to take off from a carrier. Miller established a maximum allowable take off distance of 350ft in a

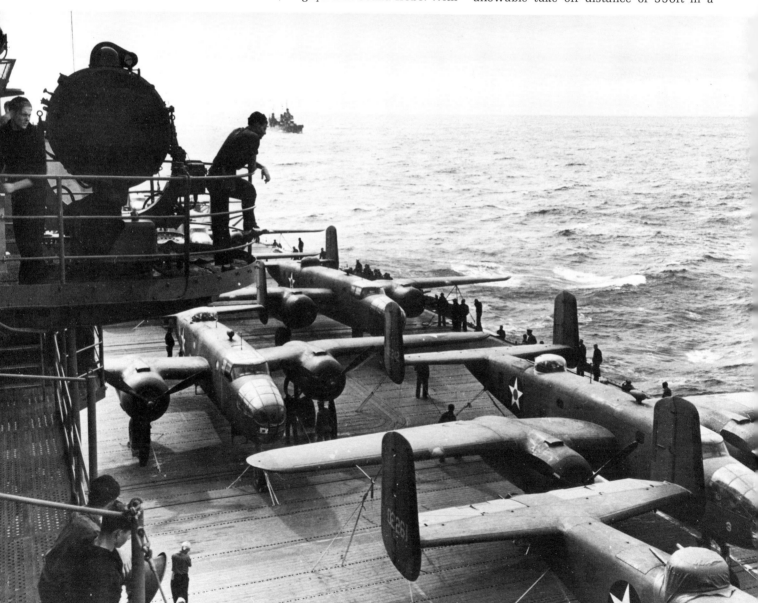

27

40kt wind at an all-up weight of 31,000lb — 2,000lb over the B-25B's design maximum. The site chosen for training was Hurlburt Field, part of the giant Eglin base complex but far enough away from inquisitive eyes.

With a yellow line down the centre of the runway helping each pilot keep his aircraft's nosewheel straight during the take off roll, the B-25s lifted off their concrete carrier. Distances were marked by flags at the side of the strip, set at 250 and 400ft, then every 50ft up to 700ft maximum. Each aircraft took off using different flap, stabiliser and power settings, the loaded weight gradually being increased as the technique was mastered. Lt Miller stationed himself behind the pilot on every take off to observe progress and prepare a

thorough critique for discussion. Fog over Eglin reduced the planned number of training days from 15 to 10, but all crews were proficient by the time they left Florida and flew to Sacramento.

Throughout the training phase, delays were caused by malfunction of the special equipment. Fuel tanks caused no end of trouble by continually leaking until finally, 225gal self-sealing tanks replaced the 265gal ones, although the fuel seepage problem was never completely eradicated. Space was also found for a third tank holding 60gal in the well provided for the retracted ventral turret. This item was removed from all Doolittle's B-25s at his instigation. When he saw how the turret was supposed to function, Doolittle commented, 'A man could learn to play the

Deck level view shows to advantage the method of tying down each B-25 — a very necessary precaution considering the weather conditions Task Force 16.2 met with. Down the deck, engine performance is checked yet again as crews go over their aircraft for the slightest hint of malfunction. There were many 'fixes' for the *Hornet's* repair shops. *USN*

28
Taken later than the previous photographs, this view shows the inboard white line painted on the flight deck to align each B-25's nosewheel during the critical take off roll. Contrary to a previous reference, it appears to confirm that the guidelines did not extend beyond the centre deck elevator positioned a few feet aft of the island. *USN*

29
So that's how the Army does it . . . Navy men watch armourers load .50-cal incendiary and tracer ammunition a short time before take off. *USN*

30
On 17 April Jimmy Doolittle delighted his men by holding an impromptu deck ceremony. He attached commemorative medals presented to US Navy men who had visited Japan in 1908 to the tail of one of the 500lb bombs his force would haul to Tokyo. *NAA*

31
Although of inferior quality, this photograph serves to show the method of spotting the Mitchells along each edge of the flight deck prior to take off. *USN*

30

31

32

32
Doolittle 'Do'od It' with yards to spare as the *Hornet* rode out a gale. The way to go was full flaps, engines to maximum power — and stabiliser in neutral. Some pilots overlooked the latter rule and a blackboard hung out from the island to give the compass heading and wind speed was quickly amended to include it.

violin good enough for Carnegie Hall before he could learn to fire that thing.'

Packed in behind the turret tank would be 10 5gal cans to top it up as fuel was used en route to the target, thus providing each aircraft with a total of 1,141gal on which to fly about 1,900miles.

More weight was saved by removing the 230lb liaison radio and the Norden bomb sight, which weighed about 45lb. Not keen to use the still-classified Norden — which was anyway of little use below 4,000ft where a short bomb run would be made and on which violent manoeuvres could be expected — Capt Ross Greening, a raider group pilot and armament officer, developed the 'Mark Twain'. This simple

sighting bar and plate device was fabricated in the Eglin workshops from materials that cost only 20 cents — a Norden cost over $10,000. The name Mark Twain was bestowed by Capt Greening; it referred to the simple 'lead line' depth finder used on Mississippi river boats in times past.

Attempting to sight the target through the Norden's optics and restricted field of vision at the intended 1,500ft attack altitude was found to be next to impossible, but the cheap substitute coped very well. Capt Greening was able to connect it to the remaining linkages that served the Norden, which permitted the bombardier to give aircraft turn directions to the pilot through

33
Seconds before the *Hornet's* bow dipped into the next wave trough, Doolittle's aircraft was clawing for altitude. *NAA*

34
Another view of Doolittle's take off technique recorded from the USS *Enterprise*. it took exactly one hour to get all 16 B-25s safely away.

33

34

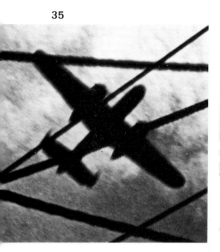

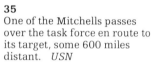

35
One of the Mitchells passes over the task force en route to its target, some 600 miles distant. *USN*

36
Co-pilot's view of numerous tempting targets in Yokosuka harbour was taken by Lt Richard Knobloch, who brought back the only photographic record of the raid subsequent to the carrier take off. Knobloch's pilot, Lt Edgar McElroy, dropped one of his bombs on the aircraft carrier *Ryuho*. *NAA*

.the PDI without relying on voice communications. Wind drift could also be set.

Prior to the bomb run, a dropping angle was computed and the sighting bar set at that angle. The bombardier then had an open field of vision over the sight to direct the pilot on to the target. When the target became aligned with the sighting bar, the bombs were released.

Greening also proposed that two 'broomstick fifties' be placed in each aircraft's tailcone, a ruse that was realistic enough from a distance, as each aircraft otherwise had only the two turret guns and a single .30-cal in the nose — hardly enough for effective defence. It was hoped though that enough surprise would be achieved for running fights with enemy fighters to be avoided.

As well as the guns themselves, gunnery caused headaches; few of the 17th Group's crews had ever fired at a moving target and there was a general lack of experience

throughout the squadrons. The turrets also had their share of problems, causing the project planners considerable frustration. More was to come when the B-25s moved to McClellan Field for final checking prior to departure from Alameda NAS.

Only 22 crews made the move to McClellan, as two B-25s had been damaged in training and had to be left behind when the force departed Eglin on 24 March, Lt Miller took crews out from McClellan for further practice take offs while personnel of the Sacramento Air Depot installed a number of items vital to the mission, including the rubber fuel tanks, covers for the bomb bay tanks and new hydraulic valves for the gun turrets. Doolittle, told that some of the equipment had not arrived, grew increasingly impatient with the casual attitude of some base personnel and was forced to resort to his highest priority orders to get things moving. One annoyance was that

37
A dejected Doolittle, convinced the raid had been a failure, sits by the wreckage of his aircraft near Tien Mu Shen, 70 miles north of Chinchow. By 20 April he had reached Chungking and wired Gen Arnold to confirm that Tokyo had been bombed. Sgt Paul Leonard, engineer-gunner in the lead crew, took the picture. Note detached propeller at top right.

39

38
Of the eight raiders who were captured by the Japanese, three were executed and one died in captivity. Lt Robert Hite, imprisoned for 40 months, was released at the end of the war. He is seen here being led blindfolded from a transport at Tokyo.

39
By far the greatest loss of life as a result of the raid was among the Chinese civilian population living in those regions where the B-25s were forced to crash land. Thousands of people were butchered by the Japanese on the pretext that they had aided the American airmen when relatively few had actually done so. Lt Knobloch's camera also recorded this group shot of (left to right) Lt Claydon Campbell, Sgt Adam Williams, Edgar McElroy and Sgt Robert Bourgeois with the Chinese who helped them evade hostile troops for several weeks after the raid.

mechanics, uninformed about the special nature of the B-25s, went about re-adjusting carburettors 'by the book' after they had been meticulously tuned to give best possible, above average performance. Doolittle finally told his pilots and crews to double check any work done on their aircraft and report anything that would adversely affect performance. Time was getting short.

When the Mitchells departed McClellan, some still with their modifications incomplete, they were at least ready for their long overwater flight, packed with extra fuel tanks, freed of their cumbersome lower turrets and with tuned engines and

new propellers. Each aircraft also had a new autopilot.

Crews taxied their machines to the dock at Alameda where fuel was drained and Navy 'donkeys' towed them to the pier. A crane swung each bomber up on to the flight deck of the *Hornet*, to be followed aboard the carrier by 70 Army officers and 64 enlisted men. At 10.18 on Thursday 2 April 1942, the Doolittle Raiders were on their way.

Rather than duplicate the well documented accounts of the *Hornet's* voyage and the raid that have already appeared in print, let the accompanying photographs tell the rest of the story . . .

Commerce Destroyer

After the disastrous opening phases of the Pacific war, the USAAF consolidated a motley collection of aircraft in Australia, established base and maintenance facilities and prepared to open a new offensive against the Japanese, using New Guinea as a forward area. A handful of B-26s, A-20s, A-24s and B-17s were undertaking necessarily limited operations when the transport USS *Ancon* docked at Brisbane on 25 February 1942 and disembarked personnel of the 3rd Bomb Group (Light). Men from the 8th, 13th and 90th Squadrons, plus the attached 89th Reconnaissance, had come without aircraft and, joining a number of ex-27th Bomb Group pilots, were placed under the command of Col John H. 'Big Jim' Davies, an exceptional leader not adverse to expedient measures to get his outfit operational. Thus the 13th and 90th Squadrons quickly acquired 15 B-25s at Archer Field near Brisbane. These were C models awaiting collection by Dutch personnel for use by No 18 (Netherlands East Indies) Squadron, which formed under RAAF control on 4 April.

The story goes that Davies informed Washington of his 'reverse Lend-Lease' move, making the theft more or less legal, although the rightful owners of the Mitchells did not protest too hard. Having suffered heavily in Java, the Dutch were understandably none too keen to regroup and return there and Davies' logical arguments, plus some assurances of financial

recompense for their aircraft, won the day. Without further delay, the Third Attack flew back to Brisbane, taking with it Jack Fox, NAA Field Representative in Australia.

Events forced such measures, for the Japanese had begun an all-out assault on remaining US and Filipino forces on Bataan on 3 April and on the 4th, Darwin was bombed again. On 5 April, the B-25 made its combat debut in the Pacific.

The target for the American bombs was Gasmata on New Britain, the small force of five aircraft of the 13th Squadron receiving only slight damage from flak, the Japanese gunners opening fire only when the raid was almost over. But let Col J. H. 'Harry' Mangan, one of the pilots on that historic mission, take up the story, quoting from a diary he kept at the time. The entry for 7 April noted:

'These last few days have been crammed to the full. The 13th has now been in actual combat in WW2. May they do even more than the 13th of WW1. On 5 April, we took off from Charters Towers, Australia and headed for Moresby. Trip over was nice despite occasional rain storms en route. About 6.30 in the evening we pulled into Moresby and, after much wheel spinning, managed to find a bed and a little food. I was rather surprised to find B-26s (22nd Bomb Group) and a stray Fortress or two (19th BG) already there.

'6 April: Up at 4.00 and to our target — Gasmata, New Britain. Battled weather

Excellent close-up of a B-25C of the 71st BS, 38th Bomb Group, at Garbutt Field, Townsville, one of the Australian airfields where 5th Air Force maintenance teams could work unmolested and fit Army bombers for the rigours of combat over New Guinea. The optional side-facing ball and socket mountings for a .30-cal gun were fairly well utilised by early Pacific theatre Mitchells before many of them received strafer nose modifications — as demonstrated here by an unidentified crewman. On 11 November 1942, the photographer got 2-Lt W. L. Uhler to take the pilot's seat with 2-Lt Don S. Hopkins as co-pilot.
AAF via Bruce Hoy

41

42

43

41
A second 11 November photo at Townsville shows 38th Group mechanics replacing the port Cyclone of *Scat*, almost certainly a 71st Squadron B-25C. *USAF*

42
With nose, turret and waist guns at the ready, six 71st Squadron Mitchells fly a practice out of Townsville on 12 November 1942. Apart from the aircraft at the extreme left, they are: B-25C 41-29708; B-25D 41-29710 *Pacific Prowler* (serial not applied at this time); B-25C 41-12895 *Grass Cutter*; B-25C 41-12890 *Pistoff* and B-25D 41-29727 *Twenty or Nothing*. *AAF via Bruce Hoy*

43
Surrounded by some of the essentials for survival and a degree of comfort off duty, this ground crew was, according to the original caption, about to load them into *Grass Cutter* at Port Moresby for a ferry flight. *USAF via Bruce Hoy*

44

Obviously awaiting an inspection (mercifully rare during the early days of the Pacific fighting) Australian and American air and ground crews of the 3rd Attack stand by their aircraft. *El Aquila*, 41-12515, was a B-25C appropriated from the Dutch and had flown 11 missions, while *Mortimer* on the left had 15 chalked up by the summer of 1942. *USAF*

45

One of the first production batch of B-25Cs lifting off from a Port Moresby aerodrome makes, simply, a good picture. It is certain though that those watching on the ground hoped more than usual that it would make a safe return, for experienced crews and B-25s were worth their weight in gold in 1942.
Australian War Memorial via Bruce Hoy

over the Owen Stanley Range and finally reached our target. We made a turn into the airfield and at 8.36 our bombs were on their way. I was rather excited but nothing like I expected. We finished the run and pulled off the target just as the Jap ack-ack was getting unusually hot. Later, after landing, we found a hole through one of the top turrets and one or two shrapnel gashes in one aircraft's tail. The gunner in the turrrret was not even scratched.

'We had five B-25s, bombed at 5,000ft in a "Vee" flight using the Norden sight, dropping on the leader. This was standard practice, giving a good ground pattern and the formation offered crew protection as well. Although our .50-cal turret guns were impressive, the .30-cal in the nose was a dog by comparison and of little value. We knew we had to change to survive.'

In order for the medium bombers to reach Japanese targets in New Guinea it was vital for the Allies to hold Port Moresby, develop the air base facilities there and launch what retaliatory raids that were possible with the equipment available. In the meantime two final missions were undertaken before the fall of the Philippines.

On 11 April, the 13th and 90th Squadrons provided 11 B-25s, mostly flown by ex-27th Group crews, and three B-17s. The force, led by Brig Gen Ralph Royce and Col Davies, flew to Del Monte and Valentia aerodromes, following the first phase of a plan that originally called for the bombers to stage through Bataan. But when Bataan fell on 9 April, the target was changed to Cebu City in the central Visaynas, about 100 miles north of the Philippines. Ten B-25s reached their intermediate destination, one aircraft having to be left behind at Darwin with a torn mainwheel tyre. The force took off at first light on 12 April and set course for the target. Sweeping low over Cebu City harbour and docks, the American flyers achieved complete surprise, only sporadic and innaccurate anti-aircraft fire being put up by the defences. In the afternoon, the Army aircraft returned to bomb Cebu and Davao and although the enemy gunners were more alert, no hits were suffered. Target damage was equally slight, despite claims to the contrary in the heat of combat.

46

One of the veterans: B-25C 41-12905 had hardly got into its stride when this photograph was taken at Port Moresby early in 1943. Converted to a strafer, *Tokyo Sleeper* added to the 26 missions marked here and flew at least 146 with the 'Green Dragons', the 38th Group's 405th Squadron. *USAF via Bruce Hoy*

47

By early 1945 *Tokyo Sleeper* had made it 136, plus nine enemy fighters and three ships. The ring and bead sight proves that a sophisticated gunsight was not necessary to put the shells in the right place ... *Frank F. Smith*

47

But time was running out for the Philippines; even as the bombers were out on their second mission, the Japanese struck the bases they had used. All US aircraft flew to Del Monte at dusk to be refuelled for the flight back to Australia, expecting another Japanese raid at any time. Bomb bay tanks were back in the B-25s around midnight and each aircraft loaded up with as many passengers as possible and took off. Nine B-25s left that night, the aircraft flown by one Paul Irvin 'Pappy' Gunn having to remain for another 48 hours because its long range tank had been destroyed in one of the air raids. Undeterred, Gunn and his crew fitted two tanks taken from a B-18 and finally made Australia on 16 April. The Philippines were all but lost, but it was not until 6 May that the last US forces on Corregidor finally capitulated.

Far East Air Force then face an awesome task; its operational area was enormous, many of its crews had only just escaped annihilation in the Philippines and Java and its aircraft had proved to be ill-equipped to meet the Japanese on anything like equal terms. Although missions had to be flown against Japanese positions in northern New Guinea, the island, including the territory of Papua, is 1,500 miles long, second only in size to Greenland and occupying a total area of 342,000sq miles. New Guinea was then ringed by enemy-occupied islands, including New Britain (14,600sq miles), Bougainville (3,880sq miles) and the archipelago of the Dutch East Indies, which totals almost two million square miles. Surrounding each land mass, the vast Southwest Pacific oceans — the Coral, Solomon and Bismarck Seas — represented a hugh chunk of the globe to be guarded by the numerically weak US and Australian Air Forces. As much of the area as possible had to be covered by aerial reconnaissance and

after the fall of the Philippines, there began a long series of overwater patrols for weary crews unused to the debilitating climate with its full range of tropical diseases. Weather over New Guinea was often a greater hazard than the enemy: low cloud and driving rain made even routine non-combat flights an exacting business and for the unwary there were the peaks of the Owen Stanley mountains, invariably shrouded in low cloud and mist and reaching to 15,000ft in places.

Bombing raids were made on the principal Japanese air bases in New Guinea — Lae, Salamua, Buna and Gona — by small formations, usually without the luxury of fighter cover. And they were occasionally disastrous. One such took place on 24 May, a fortnight or so after the Battle of the Coral Sea had forestalled Japanese attempts to land reinforcements at Moresby. Eight B-25s, six from the 3rd Group's 13th Squadron and two from the 90th, were assigned to attack Lae, about 180 miles from Moresby and which had since 8 April, been home to the Tainan

48
There were some mishaps. This B-25C swerved into the kunai grass at the edge of 14-mile strip, Moresby and did itself quite a bit of harm. The tailplane was twisted, the fuselage skin aft of the cockpit was strained and the port wheel hub lost the protection of its tyre. The B-25 didn't take kindly to belly landings and the assembled company's thoughts undoubtedly centred on how best to move the aircraft without any more damage. The dog seems to be contemplating a use for the main oleo leg . . .
USAF via Frank F. Smith

fighter wing flying the superlative Mitsubishi A6M3. Hand picked for their ability and agressiveness in combat, this group of pilots included men of the calibre of Hiroyeshi Nishizawa, Jinichi Sasai and Suburo Sakai, easily the Imperial Navy's best and among the top fighter pilots in the world at that time.

Into this hornet's nest plunged Capt Herman F. Lowery, 13th Squadron CO and his formation. The B-25s had dropped their bombs before the Zeros pounced, 11 of them against eight poorly-armed medium bombers. Lowery was singled out by Nishizawa, who needed but a short burst to explode the B-25. Toshio Ota and Sakai shot down two more and Sasai the fourth. Number five was bounced by Sakai and sent down in flames, leaving one B-25 still in the area, two having made good their escape. Although sustaining many hits, the sixth machine staggered away to put down at Moresby for a crash landing.

Such actions highlighted the weak defensive armament of the B-25C: both turrets left unprotected blind spots ahead of, below and to the side of the aircraft, which enemy pilots were quick to exploit. The lack of an extreme tail gun was also felt to be dangerous and field service units were soon rigging improved defensive positions for B-25s. And there was one man, who, with the enthusiastic support of NAA representative Jack Fox and Gen George Kenney, was to be instrumental in changing the entire concept of the B-25, giving it a totally new, highly effective role. That man was Pappy Gunn.

Born at Quitman, Arkansas (a misnomer he was powerless to correct) Gunn had, by September 1939, retired from the US Navy an above-average pilot with the rank of Chief Petty Officer. Having made his home

in Manila, he was operating a small inter-island air service when the Japanese attacked Pearl Harbor. When their bombs fell on Manila on 8 December, Gunn joined the USAAF with the rank of captain and offered his airline for military liaison flights, an offer quickly taken up. Until Christmas 1941 Gunn and his pilots flew numerous missions throughout the Philippines, delivering mail, despatches, drugs and personnel. When the Japanese took Manila in February 1942, he was forced to leave his family in the city.

Having flown some of the early missions with the 27th Group and attached himself to the 'Grim Reapers', Pappy's experience and flying ability came to General Kenney's attention. Not given to pass up talent when he saw it, Kenney made Gunn his unofficial chief test pilot. Kenney said of him, 'He wasn't a spectacular person, but spectacular things seemed to seek him out and highlighted the fact that he was different'.

Gunn and Kenney first met at Charters Towers in August 1942 where Pappy was also a maintenance and engineering officer with the 3rd Attack. The FEAF commander's preoccupation then centred on adapting the Group's A-20s to carry parafrags — 23lb fragmentation bombs dropped by parachute to explode above ground — which he believed would be highly effective against dispersed Japanese aircraft and airfield installations. The A-20s also acquired four forward-firing guns apiece to turn them into effective strafers during low altitude attacks. As the maintenance people finished each conversion, the strafers went into combat and, given the right conditions — particularly if the enemy was surprised — they achieved a high degree of success.

On 3 September 1942, the 5th Air Force was officially constituted with George Kenney commanding. The 5th assumed command of all AAF organisations in Australia and New Guinea and established areas of responsibility. Henceforward, the RAAF would provide the defence of Australia and undertake operations against the Dutch East Indies, with the 5th's jurisdiction being eastern New Guinea and its surrounding waters. Kenney then had 45 B-25s in two medium bomber groups, the 22nd and 38th — which flew its first mission on the 15th — 40 B-26s, and a roughly equal number of Mitchells and Havocs in the 3rd Attack, an inventory of 124 medium and attack bombers, 70 heavies and 250 fighters. Never were all aircraft equipped or serviceable at any one time, however. And the 5th Air Force was at the end of a 7,500-mile supply line that was stretched very thin in those days, with the prospect of little more than a trickle of replacement aircraft, crews and spares. The threat to Australia was by no means removed and New Guinea's defenders were only just hanging on.

Having weathered its 33rd air raid in April, Port Moresby became the staging area for Allied aircraft determined to prevent a seaborne Japanese invasion. Forced into New Guinea's south-western tip, Australian forces had repulsed an over-land attack from Buna and by mid-August, it was estimated that the next Japanese objective would be Moresby itself, following landings at Milne Bay. On 25 August reconnaissance confirmed the threat and combat was joined in a desperate series of actions which ended with the enemy landing a small force at Milne Bay. Constantly bombed and strafed from the air and for once outnumbered, the Japanese

failed to land further reinforcements. The Allies thus prevented the enemy employing the second prong of a pincer movement to take Port Moresby. Kenney knew that if he could deny the remaining Japanese troops in New Guinea their vital supplies, all of which had to come by sea, they could be beaten. Bombing the Japanese under their jungle canopy was proving a difficult, frustrating business with few significant results, but by September, the strafer A-20s were achieving results.

By October, Kenney was able to take the initiative and send heavy bombers to the enemy bastion of Rabaul, thereby taking some of the pressure off the Marines, then hard pressed to hold Guadalcanal. The 5th Air Force's B-17s had done sterling work since the start of the Pacific war, but their results were all too often negative. The raids helped keep the enemy's head down, but the material damage was negligible, particularly as the primary targets were very often ships, notoriously difficult to hit from high altitude.

49
The first production B-25D-10 became the 38th's *Outlaw*. It is seen here looking for trouble in company with at least one other Mitchell early in 1943. *Frank F. Smith*

50
Ole Gappy was another veteran of the 38th Group's long war over New Guinea, finishing up with 116 missions. This scene apparently shows another impending move of base, from Rorona, where the group was located from November 1942 for the desperate actions to hold Buna. Subsequently the 38th moved to Durand. *USAF via Bruce Hoy*

51
And then things changed . . . Pappy Gunn (in cockpit) and Jack Fox with the first of Kenney's 'Commerce destroyers', the strafer Mitchells that wrote a new chapter in air warfare. *NAA*

52
Mortimer's transformation: After 18 missions, one of the first B-25s to arrive in the south-west Pacific 'got the treatment' at Townsville. The nose furnishings have gone to make way for four fixed guns and slots have been cut for the ammunition feed for the twin gun side packages. Relieved momentarily of weight up front, the nosewheel leg torque link has opened to its fullest extent. *NAA*

It was the B-17s themselves which helped solve that particular problem; they still used a straight and level bomb run — but at only 250ft. Major William Benn of the 43rd BG had for some two months been perfecting a new technique and on 20 October, he led a selected group of pilots into Rabaul harbour. Enough smoke and debris filled the air to convince the B-17 crews that they had sunk a number of vessels — the fact that they had only damaged a few made no difference at a time when even a confirmed hit — let alone a sinking — on a ship was cause to celebrate. The point was that Benn, backed by an enthusiastic Kenney, had proved that low level skip bombing was the answer. And the B-17s had made the first such attack at night . . .

It was found that skip bombing required a height of 250ft at an air-speed of 200-220mph. A released bomb would thus fall 60-100ft short of the target vessel, skim off the surface of the sea and hit up to 100ft further on, skim again and hit again in the same distance. If the aircraft was correctly aligned with its target, the bomb would penetrate just above the waterline, causing extensive, if not fatal damage. Kenney had skip bombing and parafrags. He was about to get guns, double those of the A-20 strafers.

Back in Australia, Pappy Gunn's modifications were being put in hand by the various support units, among them the 8th and 45th Service Squadrons and the 81st Depot Repair Squadron, to turn standard B-25C and D models into strafers. Everything that could be removed from the bombardier's station went out to make room for the breeches and ammunition feeds of a quartet of .50-cal machine guns, set in pairs one above the other. Physically larger and heavier than the .30-cal gun, the 'fifties' needed a series of bolted bars fixed to brackets to hold them rigidly in place, over half the length of the 36in barrel and cooling jacket protruding through circular holes cut in the plexiglass. In most cases, the perspex panels were painted over.

Having made the dorsal guns capable of being locked to fire forward, Gunn and his team tried fixing three more guns under the B-25's forward fuselage and there was even talk of setting one more in each landing light bay. Jack Fox was aghast. He feared that the recoil could damage the wing spar and vetoed that particular modification on the spot.

Gunn persisted with the fuselage guns, which gave trouble due to their ammunition feed and eventually, the grouping of three weapons gave way to two on each side, the four breeches being covered by fairings or packages. Vertical ammunition chutes were fitted inside the fuselage. Blast caused a few popped rivets at first, but the solution was to move each package aft about three feet, flanking each side below the cockpit windows. Rivets still sprung despite steel plate stiffeners, sponge rubber finally being used to 'soak up' the recoil.

Some but by no means all B-25C/D strafers also acquired extreme tail defence in the form of a single .50-cal machine gun bolted down to fire through the open end of the fuselage with the transparent observation blister removed. Initially, this gun was little more than a 'scare' weapon as the prone gunner had very little rearward vision. Before too long, the modification centres built a fairing over the top of the tailplane centre-section and cut away the top of the rear fuselage to take a seat. Strafer squadrons also retained a small

number of unmodified bombardier-nosed models for use as 'lead ships'; carrying a navigator and for liaison flights and general hack work.

Kenney was delighted with the B-25 strafer, but he asked Pappy Gunn to fire off 20,000 rounds just to make sure the airframe could withstand the stress. Despite Pappy's claim to have thrown away the centre of gravity to save weight, it was well known that the B-25 could be very sensitive to any drastic weight shift. The tests completed, the prototype B-25 strafer, appropriately named *Pappy's Folly* was flown out to Moresby on 29 December 1942 for demonstration to the 90th Bomb Squadron. General Kenney's 'commerce destroyer' was ready for action.

Major 'Ed' Larner, newly-promoted CO of the 90th, quickly saw the potential of the strafer Mitchell, as did Capt 'Jock' Henerby, later to command the squadron after Larner's death. Others were a little sceptical of the flying arsenal until it had proved its worth. By February 1943, most of the 90th was equipped with strafers and working hard to perfect the dual techniques of low level attack and skip bombing, using a beached transport in Moresby's Merrick Bay as a practice target.

In the meantime, the 38th Bomb Group had flown its first mssion, on 15 September. The 71st and 405th Squadrons despatched 12 B-25Cs from Horn Island, situated off Australia's Cape York Peninsula; they staged through Moresby and carried out a medium altitude bombing attack on enemy forces in the Buna area. The following month, the group moved to Rogers Aerodrome at Rorona, New Guinea, otherwise known as '30-mile 'drome'. (The Moresby airstrips were widely referred to by their distance from the port rather than the name of the actual location.)

So bad were the living conditions at its new home that the group quickly moved an advanced echelon to Durand (17-mile) to fly missions. Almost as bad, Durand was subject to frequent Japanese bombing raids — as were all the Port Moresby airfields at that time.

For the next few weeks, the 38th undertook close support and reconnaissance sorties over New Guinea, out to Cape Gloucester and New Britain before it too

53
Decked out with a suitably ferocious paint job, *Mortimer* hides its lethal purpose from prying Japanese eyes under a camouflage net on a New Guinea dispersal. For much of its career, the aircraft was slavishly cared for by Tech Sergeant Simmons, its regular crew chief. *NAA*

54
Mortimer arrived in the Pacific on 31 March 1942 and about a year later it had flown at least 62 combat missions. During the work at Townsville, the photographer took the chance to record the gunners' enemy aircraft claims — five for the dorsal turret, two for the ventral turret, four for the bombardier using the gun from the side of the nose and one when firing from head-on. Named after Edgar Bergen's *Mortimer Snerd* cartoon character, the aircraft not only flew the first-ever B-25 mission in WW2, but also the Royce Philippine missions. It had many different crews throughout its combat career. *NAA*

55
Recommended Technique: A green-tailed 'Sun Setters' strafer making the classic skip bombing run, the pilot holding his speed a shade above 200mph, and height at 250ft. The first 500-pounder is about to hit again at bottom right of the picture, as the second bomb is dropped. *USAF via Frank F. Smith*

began to receive B-25 strafers. On 1 December, the B-25s wreaked havoc amongst enemy seaborne transport in the Buna area, and on the 14th wiped out a Japanese force attempting to put reinforcements ashore at Mambare, up the coast from bitterly contested Buna. Seven missions were flown that day, crews grabbing a quick drink and bite to eat as the ground-crews feverishly reloaded ammunition and parafrags. Such was the ferocity of the 38th's attacks that the landing party was annihilated.

More support missions were flown before the great news came through that the Allies had secured Buna, on 2 January. Subsequently the entire coast of southwest New Guinea was cleared, recaptured territory yielding the vital airfields that would be developed to launch fresh 5th Air Force offensives. In March, the bloody battle of the Bismarck Sea wrecked the last Japanese invasion force to set out for New Guinea — and the long road to Tokyo was opened. There was still a great distance to go but henceforward, there were few attempts to wrest jungle areas from the Japanese. Instead, pockets of resistance were bypassed as new areas were captured with the express purpose of establishing airfields. Based on them would be the means to stop the Japanese on land, at sea and in the air — the fighters, heavy bombers, transports and medium bombers, the most numerous of which was the B-25. Eventually distributed throughout the three full groups — the 38th, 345th and 42nd, the latter part of the 13th Air Force — and squadrons of the 22nd and 3rd Groups, plus the solitary 17th Reconnaissance Squadron, the number of B-25s was nevertheless only marginally higher than for example, in the 12th Air Force — with a very much larger operational area to control. But what Mitchell crews did to contain, then hunt down and destroy the Japanese across the Pacific battlegrounds was a major factor in Allied victory. Many B-25s piled up scores of missions and hundreds of flying hours, a record reflected in patched, oil-streaked and faded paintwork topped off by striking unit insignia — the fearsome bats, tigers, dragons and wolves that represented high espirit de corps amongst a unique group of combat flyers.

56

56
A 'Green Dragon' B-25D on patrol. One of the two full B-25 groups in the 5th Air Force, the 38th won four Distinguished Unit Citations in 35 months of combat and the only Medal of Honour award to a B-25 crewman. *Frank F. Smith*

57

57
Almost certainly B-25D 41-29697, *Junior Bat* was a 38th BG strafer retired from combat after near-total damage in 1943. Although earmarked for the boneyard, it was repaired by 5th Air Service Command and featured in a story in the May 1944 *Flying* magazine. Photos and text revealed the damage: 'The tail was mangled, the fuselage crumpled as if it had been caught in a giant vice, one nacelle was smashed and the top from the pilot's seat back to the bomb bay was chewed to pieces.' After a three month rebuild, the resulting fast transport, appropriately renamed *Patches*, served out its time on support duties. *via Bruce Hoy*

Slugging with Junior

By the time the 12th Bombardment Group arrived in the Mediterranean in the summer of 1942, the Allied position in Egypt was precariously balanced: the Afrika Korps was poised for an assault aimed at skirting the southern flank of the British 8th Army's positions and sweeping towards Alexandria. By June a stalemate had been enforced, Rommel's Panzers having been halted at El Alamein on a front stretching from the Quattara Depression to the coast, about 70 miles from Alexandria. Bernard Montgomery, determined to consolidate until his forces were rested and properly equipped for a decisive engagement, gained a vital few weeks while the Allied air forces pounded Axis airfields, ports and supply lines around the clock. Supplies had always been the key to victory in North Africa and now, if Allied airpower could deny the Germans their fuel, food, ammunition and spares, the Axis grip on the continent would be broken.

There was, therefore, precious little time for the B-25 crews of the 12th to season themselves to the conditions of desert warfare, but the slackening of activity on the ground at least allowed a month of operational training. For this the American mediums, resplendent in their 'desert pink' camouflage, joined with 3 Wing South African Air Force, otherwise composed of South African and RAF Boston and Baltimore squadrons, from 25 August. Inevitably, there was some friction when American crews thought their training superior to the operational procedures then in force. Although they had never experienced anything like the conditions in the desert, it took time to convince them that the British and South Africans knew a little more then they did. One departure for the US Mitchell crews was night raids in an

58
Able to go into action just before Rommel's last gamble in Egypt, the 12th Bomb Group was the first USAAF medium bomber group in the Mediterranean theatre. It rapidly lived up to its nickname The 'Earthquakers' and as part of the 9th Air Force, paved the way for the spectacular success achieved by medium groups in subsequent stages of the war. In this view, 'desert pink' B-25Cs of the 434th and 83rd Squadrons head out across the desert wasteland. Aircraft number 80 carries the name *Man O' War*.
Smithsonian Institution

59, 60, 61, 62
Not only did the 12th Bomb Group introduce the Mitchell to the MTO, is also showed the American perchant for humorous and sexy nose art. Most group aircraft carried at least a name and usually an appropriate painting, as these photographs show. Use of the squadron nickname was however, relatively rare. *Pluto* was a B-25C-1, 41-13167. *NAA*

aircraft not ideally suited to them. But as the 12th was under Allied command, it was obliged to join in the nocturnal attacks which had long been standard practice for British light bomber units. The main problem was the bad flame damping properties of the single engine exhaust of the B-25C, a point stressed by A&AEE Boscombe Down when the first examples of this model arrived in the UK.

Roy Woods, a pilot with the 12th Group's 434th Squadron recalls those early days and some of the challenges to be faced:

'I was co-pilot to the squadron CO on the early night missions; the single exhaust stack was a good target and we lost some ships and crews before exhaust rings with stacks for the individual cylinders were installed early in the campaign. Our

bombing altitude was initially anything up to 10,000ft, until British and South African statistics indicated fewer hits by flak at altitudes between 8-10,000ft. We accordingly varied between those heights as B-25 engines required the use of a high blower above 10,000ft.

'Sand was a problem, but not really evident until the sand screen (filter) was removed for a special mission to Crete — many engines were damaged while warming up took place and it was not a successful mission. The filters were removed to supposedly get more distance from the standard gas load.

'The number of planes we took off at one time really depended on how close we were to the nearest Jerry encampment. It varied, as I recall, from three to 12 or 18 at a time. We flew formations during daylight raids and dropped on indication from the lead navigator, initially using only bomb bay racks but later, approximately midway through our desert service, auxiliary wing racks were added too.'

Under the command of Col Charles Goodrich, the 'Earthquakers' gradually came to terms with the deprivations of their new combat area and by mid-August the group had occupied two airfields in the Nile delta — the 81st and 82nd Squadrons at Deversoir and the 83rd and 434th at Ismalia. During its training period, the 12th flew night raids to the port of Matrah and Axis airfields at Daba and Fuka and gave able support to the Allied effort to check Rommel, who made a bid to break the stalemate on 30 August. In six days, the group flew 47 sorties.

On 3 September, the 12th flew 18 sorties against retreating Axis columns, having lost its first aircraft on the 1st. In company with Allied Bostons and Baltimores, the American Mitchells began to establish a fine reputation for accurate bombing by day, but by night it was of debatable value to send them out, as their bright exhaust flames acted as a beacon to flak and fighters. Even before the Alamein battle, a recommendation had been made that the B-25s be flown at night 'only in extreme emergencies'. And on the night of 13/14 September the reason became abundantly clear; four B-25s failed to return from a six aircraft mission to Sidi Hanaish aerodrome. Among the losses was the aircraft flown by Col Goodrich, who became a PoW.

By the end of September, the 12th had completed 21 missions, dropped 139 tons of bombs and lost six aircraft. There followed a period of relative calm as the group, in common with the rest of the Allied bomber force, prepared for the forthcoming air offensive to support a counter attack. As a direct result of the 12th's difficulties in mounting effective night sorties, US combat units assigned to theatres of British responsibility were organised into 'homogenious American formations', USAMEAF bombers coming under British control only for strategic purposes. This welcome change took effect from 12 October.

Col Edward N. Backus took command of the 'Earthquakers' as the group undertook a series of missions, mainly against enemy airfields, prior to the big offensive. The group moved base to LG88 to be nearer the battlelines and became part of 232 Wing RAF, both the mediums and the P-40s of the 57th Fighter Group having their activities co-ordinated when the US Desert Air Task Force was activated on 22 October.

The night of 19/20 October 1943 saw the start of the massive air effort with a three-fold purpose: to deny the enemy air reconnaissance and the ability to interfere with the Allied advance to destroy supplies and communications in the Tobruk-Sollum area; and to sap the morale of enemy troops by keeping them awake with round the clock sorties over their lines. For 48 hours hundreds of sorties were flown as a curtain raiser to the great Alamein artillery barrage which opened on the night of the 23rd. By then, most of the Axis landing grounds within range of the battlefield had been heavily bombed and as the troops advanced, they could see solid formations of Bostons, Kittyhawks, Baltimores and Mitchells overhead. The 12th's contribution was some 300 sorties between 19 and 31 October, for the loss of two B-25s.

63
Contemporary photographs indicate that the 'Earthquakers' operated more or less standard aircraft for a good few months, B-25C-1 41-13120 of the 434th even retaining its lower turret in November 1942. The twin underwing bomb racks can just be discerned.
Roy Woods via Norm Taylor

63

Such was the effectiveness of the air umbrella that the German troops had little support from the Luftwaffe during the critical phase of the battle. Rommel gradually pulled his armour back until by November it was clear that he would never again make substantial gains. The tide had turned.

So rapid was the Allied advance that by 19 November, when the British entered Benghazi, the 12th Bomb Group was out of range of its potential targets and was stood down for a period of training. On the 12th of the month, MEAF had become the 9th AAF and the 12th Group became part of IX Bomber Command when it was established on the 17th. Another move of base took the group to the satellite aerodromes of Gambut, Libya.

On 2 December, the 310th Group made its Mediterranean debut as part of the 12th Air Force, formed to support the Operation Torch landings in Northwest Africa. The second Mitchell unit to see combat in the MTO, the 310th's flight echelon made its way to England via the North Atlantic ferry route. Collecting new aircraft at Westover, Mass, the group's 54 B-25Cs flew to Presque Isle, then Goose Bay, Bluie West One and Reykjavik, Iceland. All aircraft arrived safely although when following groups experienced losses due to bad weather, other twin-engined bomber groups came by the southern ferry route.

Having itself weathered a Luftwaffe attack on Hardwick, the 310th departed England's shores for Morocco, where all four squadrons (the 379th, 380th, 381st and 428th) occupied Mediouna airfield.

The 12th Group also saw a brief spell of action in December as the 8th Army prepared to assault El Aghelia.

The Mitchells used the forward base at Magrun from 11 December, the group flying a small number of missions from the field, noted for a preponderance of mud. Again the targets were Axis airfields, supply centres and troop concentrations. P-40s covered 18 B-25s on 15 December when the American machines joined RAF Bostons and Baltimores in an attack on the coast road west of Marble Arch. A concentration of enemy motor transport suffered heavily as a result.

By mid-December, the entire 12th Group was at Gambut 3 and 4 and two days into

64

Forming up for take off, two aircraft were wrecked in a collision. Maintenance facilities were stretched when 50 engines, clogged with sand due to removal of their filters, had to be changed. Montgomery began his drive on Tripoli on 15 January and by the end of the month, the 'Earthquakers' had flown 91 MTO missions, delivering 713 tons of bombs in 744 sorties for the loss of ten aircraft.

In the meantime, hampered somewhat by lack of aircraft, the 310th was also making its mark. Having

1943 it despatched 11 aircraft for a long range strike to Crete. This was the mission mentioned earlier by Roy Woods and which resulted in the loss of two B-25s. Only the 81st and 82nd squadrons participated, as the 83rd and 434th were obliged to ride out a severe sand storm.

moved to Telergma in December, the group was using its second Algerian base by January 1943 and was involved in the support missions for Allied troops hard pressed by the Afrika Korps at Kasserine. Rommel, having been forced to concentrate his remaining forces in Tunisia, calculated that the fortified Mareth Line would hold long

66

65

65
An exploding bomb caused this crackup of 42-32309, a B-25C-10 of the 486th BS, 340th Group, at Hergla, Tunisia on 6 July 1943. One of the underwing bombs failed to drop clear until the aircraft touched down on return from a mission. The resulting jolt was enough and it detonated just behind the aircraft. *Howard Levy*

66
A formation take off by Mitchells of the 387th Squadron, Hergla, 10 July 1943. All aircraft have four 250lb bombs on the underwing racks and typical markings of the period, including an RAF fin flash as theatre identification. *Howard Levy*

67
Long service B-25C of the 321st Bomb Group *Oh-7* flew at least 74 missions three more than marked on here. The letters and number were bright red. *Richard L. Ward*

68
Whereas other theatres tailored the Mitchell to their own particular requirements, the Mediterranean groups used the aircraft almost exclusively in its designated role. Consequently, a primary concern of the 9th and 12th Air Force groups was the provision of adequate defence against fighter attack, particularly from the side and rear quarters. This need generated a variety of field modifications, examples of which are shown here. B-25C 41-12947 has large unglazed waist windows complete with an external bracing strip. The tailcone has a single .50-cal gun and there is a fairing over the tailplane centre section, believed also to have been for strengthening.
Michael O'Connor

enough for him to launch a decisive counter-attack. His plan started with a breakthrough at Kasserine Pass, Panzers and seasoned infantry sweeping through positions held by green US and French troops. But it was a desperate gamble, reliant as the Germans were on men and material from Sicily without command of the air. And in mid-January, the 12th AF directed its medium bombers and long range fighters to step up anti-shipping strikes.

By then the 310th had something of a reputation or this kind of work — so much so that none other than Jimmy Doolittle visited the group to see how true the stories were and signed himself up for a mission on 10 February. The intrepid leader of the Tokyo raid was not disappointed. The 310th's B-25s went out and sank three Siebel ferries. Ten days later, an even

bigger prize was offered — a 10,000 ton tanker escorted by a cruiser and two destroyers en route for Tunisia. Six 310th aircraft swept in in two elements at 100ft altitude. The tanker received direct hits from the first element while the following three B-25s went after the escort. With the tanker ablaze, the cruiser sinking stern first and both destroyers damaged the Mitchells withdrew, one machine having taken gunfire. This aircraft crash-landed at Bone, Algeria while a second was forced down at sea. Happily, the entire crew was rescued after spending 24 hours in their dinghy.

While Rommel made his desperate gamble, the two US medium groups added their weight to isolating his forces. B-25s were sent against strong points, rail yards and bridges as well as shipping. By the 23rd, the German attack was finally contained with Allied air strength gradually building up for the operations ahead.

The two groups that would fly the B-25 in the MTO for the rest of the war went operational within a few weeks of each other in the spring of 1943. The first was the 321st, which flew the southern ferry route from DeRidder airbase, Louisiana to Oran, via Florida, Brazil and Dakar. Beforehand, the group's B-25Cs had their lower turrets removed at Mobile, Alabama. Waist gun positions were cut in the fuselage sides and a single .50 positioned in the extreme tail for use by the flight engineer, one 321st historian recalling that it was the first time such modifications had been made throughout a B-25 combat group destined for North Africa. By mid-

68

March, the 321st had its squadrons ensconced at Ouijda, Morocco.

By the end of March, the 340th Bomb Group was at Kabrit, Egypt, everyone involved in the move from the USA thankful that all aircraft had survived some of the worst weather imaginable during the flight leg across the Atlantic. It would not have surprised some if the elements had conspired to bring the 340th more bad luck, for there was an understandable feeling that Mother Nature had it in for the 340th. Twice the group had had most of its aircraft wrecked by cyclone force winds that hit its South Carolina bases during the summer of 1942 and few things were more guaranteed to generate a 'hard luck' feeling. More, unfortunately, was to come. Meanwhile, Col William C. Mills prepared his group for action. Before March was out, the 340th teamed up with the 12th Group and provided several aircraft for a mission on the 31st. It was an unhappy debut to combat as one B-25 was lost along

with an 'Earthquaker' ship, although a second 340th machine, initially reported missing, made a late return after putting down at a forward fighter base.

Moving to Medenine in Tunisia during the first weeks of April, the 340th laid on its first full group mission on the 19th, a raid on Kourba South landing ground. Most medium bomber operations were at that time in support of the 8th Army's assault on the Mareth line and the newcomers quickly gained experience and a reputation for bombing accuracy. By the 23rd the group mounted its second full mission, misfortune striking when two B-25s collided on take off. Two more were lost on the 26th and on 2 May, Col Mills' aircraft was shot down over Furnay, Tunisia. Command passed to Lt Col Adolph E. Tokaz, who would lead the group until January 1944.

Missions continued as the enemy grip on North Africa grew ever weaker and when the end came with the Axis surrender on

69
The proud record of the 12th Bomb Group personified by *Desert Warrior*, which went home with a crew made up of personnel from each of the four squadrons, plus a Canadian air gunner, for a war bond tour. With 78 missions and descriptive map on the port side, the aircraft had a large scroll under the cockpit on the starboard side, plus listings of recipients of decorations from the Silver Star through Air Medal. Accompanying the Mitchell on its fund-raising flights was the B-24D *The Squaw* from the 98th Bomb Group, just visible in the background. *NAA*

18 May, the 340th had earned a DUC for the quality of its close-support bombing. In less than two months' fighting it had flown 898 sorties and returned the highest bomb tonnage dropped by the four B-25 groups during the period.

Before the invasion of Sicily, USAAF mediums joined with heavies and fighters for Operation 'Corkscrew', the neutralisation of Pantellaria. Heavily fortified to impede an Allied advance northwards, the island did not justify a time consuming and possibly costly invasion and with virtual total command of the air, Spaatz left this particular thorn to be reduced by airpower alone. Both the 340th and 12th had bombed Pantellaria on 9 May and several succeeding days, but the main offensive began on the 18th. For the next 19 days every effort was made to put at least 50 bomber and fighter sorties over the island's most important targets, especially the airfield, port installations and flak positions. Backed by an effective naval blockade, the Allied air units moved closer to their targets, the 12th and 340th occupying Hergla, Tunisia from 2 June. There work was put in hand to rectify some of the operational shortcomings of the latter group's aircraft, principally in armament. The majority of C models then in service had the inadequate 'Stateside' armament, including the lower turret. And in most cases, there was no extreme tail defence. Most of the ventral turrets were therefore removed and new waist positions made, together with a single .50 tail gun and new gunsights.

Until 10 June the mediums pounded Pantellaria and along with two groups of B-17s, dropped over 40,000 tons of bombs. On the 11th Allied landing craft were able to go ashore to be received by an exhausted garrison, shattered and demoralised by the carpet of high explosive laid across the island. B-25s also helped persuade Lampedusa that further resistance was useless and three days after Pantellaria fell, the rest of the Pelagic islands surrendered.

Sicily was the next objective and the bombers' targets included airfields and installations by day and night in preparation for the invasion. Allied forces went ashore on 10 July and made rapid progress under the air umbrella. On 2 August, advance parties arrived at Comiso to patch up Allied bomb damage and by the 3rd, the base was accommodating most of the 340th's B-25s. They continued to give excellent close support and by 18 August, Sicily had been secured. Such was the quality of the group's bombing in support of the US 7th Army that it received a DUC.

In October 1943, a month after attention focused on the pre-invasion bombardment of Italy, the 9th AF relinquished its sole B-25 group to the 12th Air Force under a major reshuffle of AAF groups in the MTO. All existing and new medium bomber units henceforward came under the 12th's operational control as the 9th moved to England to regroup for the invasion of Europe.

70
An 'Earthquakers' B-25D with the same modifications shown in the previous photograph seen at Hergla, Tunisia, on 17 June 1943. The slightly bulged and braced tailcone was similar on many of the group's early aircraft. *Howard Levy*

71
Another variation on the upgunning exercise on a B-25-30 shows B-25H/J-type waist windows and fairing over a tail gunner's seat. The tail gun has a circular section of armour plate fixed at the end of the barrel cooling jacket. *Howard Levy*

70

71

Secret Weapon
Al Behrens

The great success of the modified B-25 strafers led North American to experiment with much heavier firepower from one cannon rather than a number of machine guns. Thus B-25C 41-13296 was taken from the Inglewood production line and extensively reworked to accommodate a 75mm M-4 cannon. Although this adaptation of the Army 75mm field piece was not the largest shell gun ever fitted to an aircraft — the Italians claimed that particular distinction with a 102mm weapon married to the Piaggio P108 heavy bomber of 1943 — it was certainly the largest used operationally. Neither was NAA alone in attempting to meet a War Department circular requirement for large-calibre shell guns for twin-engined aircraft, for installations were made by other manufacturers, notably Douglas with an experimental installation in a B-18 and later the A-26, but in the event, only the B-25 brought the 75mm gun to operational status.

As originally modified, the XB-25G, the first Mitchell to bear an experimental designation, had its glazed nose deleted and a solid section two feet shorter substituted to take the breeches of two .50in machine guns and the extreme end of the cannon blast tube. The breech and cradle extended back along the port side crawlway previously used by the bombardier to reach the pilot's position.

The XB-25G made its first flight on 22 October 1942, with Ed Virgin in the left hand seat. Air-to-air firing tests with the cannon proved that the addition of almost a ton of weight had little detrimental effect on the aircraft's handling characteristics, although production B-25Gs had a tendency to sink very fast if engine power was allowed to drop. According to one pilot, 'you had about seven seconds — after that it was gone'.

Cannon recoil was absorbed by a hydromatic spring device, the discharge of a shell being felt in much the same way as a car engine "coughing" on a cold morning. Unrestrained, the 75mm M-4 would recoil 21in.

Each 26in long shell was manually loaded from a 21-round magazine located behind the flight deck on the port side; each round weighed 20lb-15lb for the projectile and 5lb for the casing — or the equivalent of 78 .50-cal bullets. As production progressed, the pilot had a standard fighter type optical reflector sight, plus the ring and bead and two of the nose 'fifties to mark 'fall of shot'.

As the B-25G entered combat, reports showed a need for lengthening the barrel of the cannon by about 3in to prevent muzzle blast rupturing adjacent rivets and loosening panels. The longer barrel was fitted to the last 400 B-25C-20s completed as B-25Gs on the NA-96 contract and five B-25C-15s were also completed as service trial G models. The ventral turret was retained on the first 221 B-25Gs but deleted on subsequent machines.

Opinions as to the operational value of the 75mm varied; it was particularly well liked by crews of the 38th Bomb Group of the 5th Air Force and the 7th Air Force's 41st Group used it to very good effect — in

72
Take one artillery piece and one twin-engined medium bomber, remove the bombardier's quarters and all his gear from the latter, install the former — and you have a B-25G, heaviest cannon-toting operational aircraft of WW2. Mounted on its cradle, which was bolted to the floor of the aircraft, this example of the M-4 cannon demonstrates how the shell handling tray was mounted at the rear of the breech for direct loading. A large oil reservoir on top of the barrel called a 'recuperator' damped the recoil and a spring loaded four-petal barrel cap (shown closed here) prevented ingress of dust. *NAA*

72

73
An NAA technician cradling a single 75mm shell makes one appreciate how few targets could stand up to a few dozen of them being pumped out by low flying bombers. Many pilots (usually without the benefit of a comprehensive gunnery course) learned to use the cannon to very telling effect. *NAA*

74
There was ample room for the 75mm in the crawlway previously used by the bombardier to reach the B-25's flight deck, although the recoil could make dents in the cannoneer's knees! The petal section barrel cap was removed once the gun was secured in the aircraft. *NAA*

fact the cannon-armed Mitchells found very widespread use. It really depended on the type of target; for some, there was undoubtedly a big advantage in the batteries of forward-firing .50-cal machine guns, not least of which was that far more ammunition could be carried. On the other hand, there were few targets that would stand the pulverising from direct hits from the cannon. In the final analysis, success often depended on the technique employed and the skill of individual crews.

Al Behrens flew 49 missions as a pilot with the 822nd Bomb Squadron of the 38th Group, the famed 'Sun Setters'. Not all of them involved combat as there were courier and weather reconnaissance flights into combat zones credited as part of the total. He flew both C/D versions and the cannon-armed B-25G and 'came back without even a scratch':
'Before going into combat in October 1943, our squadron spent some time in Hawaii, during which the lower turrets of our B-25s were removed. Unlike the upper turret where the gunner had a clear view of the area he could sweep, moving with his guns, the damn Bendix was very bad. In its place the aircraft were modified to take a .50-cal gun on each side.
'Many of us felt vulnerable in B-25s that had no rear defence — we had no tail stingers at that time — so we got the ordnance people to remove the clear piece

at the end of the fuselage and rig twin .30s on a pivot mount and install the tracks and guides for two ammunition boxes on either side. The radio operator would usually man these guns while the flight engineer took care of those in the waist and we felt a little better having something in the back. Most of our missions were low level and it was comforting to know that your tail was covered as the top turret had some blind spots due to the twin tail assembly. The later H and J models had a regular tail position which covered that area real well.
'The first bombing mission I ever flew on was on 16 October 1943, a four hour 23 minute flight to Alexishaven. According to my records, we bombed, shelled and strafed dispersal areas and apparently hit an anti-aircraft position; we fired seven 75mm shells and dropped seven 300lb bombs. The next was on 23 October, to Bogadjim road west of Alexishaven. There we bombed a strafed the road and the town, hitting a tent area and also dropped seven 300 pounders. No cannon shells were used. Duration of this flight was four hours, 35 minutes at an average speed of 220-240mph.
'An interesting point about the 75mm cannon was that it was classified as a secret weapon while we were in the New Guinea area and we were not allowed even to get rid of the spent shell casings. Even though there was a chute for the purpose in the cannoneer's compartment, there was a

complete ban on using it since the Japs were not sure exactly what type of weapon we had. I remember the evening transmissions from Hollandia — which was Japanese HQ before we took it — when a typical ''Tokyo Rose'' voice would talk to us, play home town music and come across with some rather startling information, like the name of our CO and so on. She also indicated that the enemy was offering natives in the area and any of the own personnel a reward if they were to capture any of the pilots or crews of the ''aircraft that threw bombs''.

'As a consequence of this were were not allowed to eject the shells — which became something of a problem for the cannoneer. On a long run in, firing the cannon from far out, or where we made two or three passes on a target, quite a few casings would accumulate in his compartment and he would soon be above ankle deep in rattling brass. Incidentally, the 75mm cannon never was declassified, even after it was removed from the aircraft and at no time did we eject a spent casing.

'The main reason for removing the cannon was the deteriorating effects it had on the airframe, particularly around the wing leading edge close in at the root, where rivets would pop, and also along the cannon (left) side of the fuselage. Loosened and popped rivets were constantly being replaced; although at the time, we were not aware of the extent of the damage and the amount of repair work involved.

'The B-25 was constantly nose heavy with the cannon installed; the gun weighed about 1,400lb which was all forward of the centre of gravity and a great deal of nose-up trim had always to be applied in order to keep the aircraft flying straight and level. I don't know whether the cannon weight was the reason, but we did have a lot of wear and tear on nosewheels and also the dampers, the hydraulic shocks. The B-25 always looked like it was going downhill when sitting in a revetment because of the extreme weight.

'The only sighting the original B-25s had for the cannon was a regular ring and post, with no means of mechanically changing for elevation and so on. The reflector sight that was fitted when we got overseas did have a range adjustment knob so that when estimating range, we could ''dial it

75

76

75
Tiny Targets: Al Behrens noted that he missed this bridge on Bogadjim road twice. Many Japanese targets were very well concealed and even an exposed bridge like this one only gave the pilot scant seconds to sight and fire when the approach was at less than 100ft. With the B-25G the method was to open fire with the cannon, then strafe with .50-cal and finally, drop the bombs. *Behrens*

76
Prey on the waters: The Japanese employed numerous tspes of small craft to move supplies between occupied islands and beat the blockade imposed by the Allied air forces. These shallow-draught 'Sugar Dogs' have been caught by prowling 38th Group Mitchells. *Behrens*

49

77

78

77
And then there were airfields: Madang, located on the north Pacific coast of New Guinea about midway between Lae and Wewak, was quite a pleasant place for an air base, and might have remained that way had not the Allies hung on in New Guinea. As it was, the base suffered the attentions of 5th AF mediums during 1943. On one raid, Al Behrens' aircraft went out to ruin a taxiway and the strike camera recorded one bomb ploughing into the right hand side and a second about to hit on the left. *Behrens*

78
A second pass over Madang revealed this view of the airfield with little sign of life among the shattered hulks of Ki-48 'Lily' and Ki-49 'Helen' bombers. Many aircraft were disabled by blast damage from exploding bombs dropped from high altitude. *Behrens*

in'' and the compensation was there. Then it was a matter of following through as we got closer to the target. The reflector sight was of the "Christmas tree" type on which we made visual adjustments. Watching the hits and explosions of the shells also gave you the opportunity to correct, over or under.

'I should perhaps point out that a good part of our training overseas with the reflector sight was in range estimation, but since we had no mechanical or optional range finders on the aircraft, it was standard procedure to fly to an area, pick out a given target or a well recognised object and make runs on it at a given attack speed. The pilot would sing out what he thought the ranges were as he closed in and the navigator, who also doubled as the cannoneer, used a stop-watch to figure out the actual range. This method was rather crude — it would have been a lot better if someone could have told the pilot the actual ranges. He could then have automatically made his sighting "down the tree". But we had quite a bit of practice and got to be pretty effective.

'As far as I was concerned, the cannon did a real fine job the way we used it. I also think that against tanks or armoured vehicles and columns of trucks it might have been even better. But targets in the Pacific theatre were rather few and far between. None of them was very exposed, particularly trucks and jungle roads — most of the time we couldn't see the road at all. It was very effective against shipping; the barrage tactics we used were to me really something else — devastating. The target was completely covered from seven miles out and right in until we were over it. But it was probably just that type of attack that caused the cannon to be removed because once the firing started and the lead ship had made his two ranging shots, the rest of us would just fire as fast as we could. And that rapid fire had a real deteriorating effect on the airframes.

'There were no cannon misfires as I recall. We did have a problem though, with dented shell cases and it became standard practice on the way to the target for all squadron navigator/cannoneers to take each and every shell out of the rack, put it into the cannon block and close and breech to make sure it would go in and eject properly. Each one was then put back in the rack. Any casing that did not go in easily or eject properly was set aside. That way we didn't exactly solve the problem, but we did get round it.

'I can tell you that in many cases the way the ordnance people operated left a lot to be desired, particularly in the handling of belted .50-cal ammunition. We had instances where they dragged the belts along the ground to the airplanes and gave us our biggest cause for complaint — jammed machine guns. There's nothing worse than having six or eight guns to use and come over of target with only two of them operating and no time to recharge. Sometimes we had a little thing going with the ordnance people . . .

'We found that the cannon was more precise than a bomb for some targets, particularly bridges. The supply roads over the hills were only two-lane dirt tracks for most of the way, but occasionally they had to cross a small ravine or stream. A small bridge between 25 and 50ft long is not a very big target when you're making a sighting run from more than a mile away at treetop height of 50-70ft, but the 75mm gave us the opportunity of getting off anything from 3-10 rounds before we were too close in. Then we would start .50-cal strafing, winding up by toggling out whatever bombs we carried — mostly anti-personnel 300 pounders with 15sec delay fuses or 250 pounders.

'The last mission where the Black Panthers utilised the cannon was 10 January 1944, a strike to Bogadjim road. We shelled, strafed and bombed the supply road and bridges, expended nine 75mm shells and dropped seven 300lb bombs. After this, all my subsequent missions were logged at either low level strafing or medium altitude bombardment, using conventional B-25s from 7-10,000ft, missions which, inicidentally, I hated. They scared me to death because of all the flak the enemy could throw around for much longer than when we made low level attacks.

'One other weapon we used was the parafrag bomb, weighing 23lb. The bomb bay of a B-25 could take three of these anti-personnel bombs on each rack, although that still left plenty of room in the bay. Pappy Gunn, who was constantly looking for ways to improve our firepower, came up with the "squirrel cage". This was a metal rack that looked just like a cage with columns of rods. It held parafrags in fours stacked one on top of the other, nose to tail. I recall that the cage carried about 200 23 pounders and the idea was that when you were over a target you toggled the whole lot. In theory, once the lower bomb in the stack went, the other three would follow, from the rear stacks forward, until the cage was empty. It didn't work very well; the cage needed a complicated arrangement of levers and cables to release the bombs and there were instances of the little parachutes opening before bombs left the cage. They would hang up and flap and bang against the bottom of the aircraft.

'Fortunately, no aircraft was lost because of this problem, but it got so bad that men were scared to fly such missions. Many of them would drop the whole rig — when you hit the salvo button, the whole damn cage would come out. They lost so many cages that they finally gave up the idea.

'There were plenty of stories concerning Pappy Gunn and his well known passion to hit the Japanese with anything we had. Naturally, not everyone agreed with his ideas. I heard a rumour that someone even got so incensed with the danger Gunn created for the crews had a couple of sticks of dynamite were put under his cot. If it hadn't been for someone shouting a warning . . .

'But in his determination to deliver more and more destruction to the enemy, Gunn made the B-25 the instrument to do it — and I have to admit that he could really fly that thing. At one time he accepted a challenge from a P-40 pilot — another Colonel, I guess. The P-40 was ancient as we didn't have too many of them at that time, but Gunn flew rings round it. It was hard to believe he could do it with a medium bomber, but do it he did. He had so many hours in the aircraft and knew it so well that he could make it do just about anything. This particular B-25 wasn't a combat aircraft, had no bomb load or anything, but it was quite an aerial display for us to watch.

'Our shipping targets ranged from freighters to small tugs and barges. Tugs would tow anything from three to ten barges and keep right into the coastline. We didn't fly any night missions, so most enemy movement was at night or in the late afternoon when they were pretty sure we were not flying. During the day they would pull the barges up into the shore along with the tugs and try to camouflage them as best they could with coconut palms.

'Consequently, when we made a barge sweep — which happened once or twice a month — we would send a single ship and ferret them out as targets of opportunity. These missions were usually very effective and in most cases we made two or three runs when we found a concentration of boats or barges tied up along a beach.

'The largest vessel I was involved with was a small freighter escorted by a corvette. Three freighters were sighted while we were on a bombing raid and the information was radioed back. When we returned from our mission, which did not include an attack on the shipping, we were

fed at the flightline, the aircraft were refuelled and rearmed and had bombs put on and we were sent right back up again to get those ships. The freighters were about two-thirds the size of our liberty/victory ships and all three were sunk by low level bombing and cannon attacks.

'Skip bombing was the most effective method of sinking ships, because if you could get through the firepower they threw up, it was pretty much of a sure thing provided that you could just get close enough to let the bomb hit the water, as you had a large margin of error. The bomb would be released really prematurely, aiming directly at the target; if you were a little off you would still usually get a direct hit. A bit short and the bomb would hit the water, skip and still hit the target. Even if you dropped close, the bomb would tend to go in amidships and you still ended up with a hit.

'Among the non-shipping targets were airfields. We would attempt to destroy any aircraft on the field and lay enough bombs along the runways to make them inoperable for a period of time, as well as gather enough visual information as to where supply depots or gas dumps might be for our debriefing, so that another mission could be laid on to hit more specific targets.

'When we were operating out of Port Moresby, Wewak was the biggest Jap stronghold. We used to make runs up there quite often because Wewak was also the beachhead for their supplies. It had the biggest airfield with one of the highest concentrations of aircraft, it being from that area that all smaller bases were supplied with both men and equipment, ammunition and so on. Wewak was a round trip or three hours 35 minutes according to my log book. Allowing for 3-5 minutes over the targets, we're talking about an hour 45 minutes each direction.

'Other places we attacked were Gastmata, Madang, Borgan Bay, Kaidor, Kiari and Bogadjim road. Wewak was hit from Moresby and we also went to Hollandia and some of the other islands from there. We operated out of Moresby until 6 March 1944, when the whole squadron moved to Nadzab. By then we had in effect neutralised most of the airfields within striking distance of Port Moresby.

'The longest mission I show in my log book occurred on 22 June 1944, when we were based on Hollandia. We went to an island called Jackman after destroyers had been reported in the area escorting a supply ship. We were assigned to sink the freighter, but because of the range, we only had fighter cover for about three quarters of the way. We had long range tanks installed in the bomb bay, so only half the space was utilised by bombs. The mission took us seven hours, 50 minutes and I recall that I lost a wingman.

'I was shot down on 15 November 1943. It was during a mission to Wewak with about 85 B-25s participating. We were supposed to pick up our fighter escort over Gusap about 50 miles north of Nadzab, then the most advanced American base where we had fighters. I was flying the No 3 position in the last element.

'When we arrived at the rendezvous we began circling at 9,000ft, waiting for the fighters. We were flying in formation, which means that you concentrate on the No 1 ship all the time. All of a sudden there was a terrible explosion back in the navigator's compartment and the aircraft filled with smoke, I didn't know then exactly what had happened and assumed there had been a malfunction of some kind, but we decided to land at Gusap as the navigator was pretty badly hurt and bleeding.

'As we came over Gusap I looked down — and saw a string of bombs go right across the field and wondered where the heck they had come from. I looked up. A whole formation of Jap bombers had dropped their loads at the very moment we arrived and started to circle! Actually the sky up above was pretty well loaded, with Japanese bombers in formation and fighters whipping all over the place — apparently some Zeros were mixing it with our P-40s and P-38s. It was quite a sight.

'But my main concern was to get down and find some medical attention for my navigator; meantime I found out that I had no throttles. The pitch control also went

wild, the props ran away and there was no way I could reduce or increase power. The Gusap runway was in bad shape but I figured that somewhere down there I would find first aid — if I could land by going round the bomb craters.

'As we came round to make a final approach and dropped the gear, we found that it wouldn't extend fully. We had to make a go-around without being able to add power while attempting to put the gear down by emergency hydraulic pressure. That failed and we then found that the mechanical system was inoperable too. We later found the whole gear assembly completely destroyed by a shell exploding amidships.

'Our only other recourse was to fly back down to Nabzab, which had just been taken over by US forces and was being prepared for us to move up from Moresby. We decided to do that and of course made a belly landing. We tore the airplane up pretty bad, but we got the navigator out and into hospital. He subsequently recovered and went back on active duty.

'The story had an interesting sequel; on 30 November our CO called me aside and told me he'd been looking at some combat motion pictures taken by a P-40. They showed his tracers going into the belly of a B-25 over Gusap that same day and the pilot claimed he mistook us for a Jap bomber. The CO was convinced that a P-40 had shot us down. I had the answer for him. After we'd crash landed, gotten Pete to the hospital and calmed ourselves down, we went back to get some things out of the aircraft — what was left of it. We found a lot of small calibre bullet holes — not the size made by .50-cal — in the wings. They

79
These 'Black Panther' B-25G-1s came off the production line consecutively and stayed together. The decorated aircraft, 42-64812, leads its slightly older stablemate, 42-64811, over inhospitable jungle terrain, both aircraft having had their 75mm cannon removed and at least four .50-cal machine guns installed. *Behrens*

80
Any Crash You Can Walk
Away From . . . with the gear
wrecked by an exploding shell
(although he was unaware of
that fact at the time) Al
Behrens made an emergency
landing at Nadzab on
15 November 1943, mainly to
get medical help for his
wounded navigator. As he
said, 'We tore the airplane up
pretty bad . . .' *Behrens*

81
Al Behrens and fellow
lieutenants Welden (left) and
Hamilton in front of an 82nd
B-25G with typical nose gun fit
to make up for the loss of
75mm firepower. As well as
four guns mounted where
production G models had two,
a fifth .50-cal occupied the
cannon blast tube. *Behrens*

81

were of the .25-cal used by the Japs' machine guns and there were also two large holes made by explosive shells from cannon. It was standard procedure for the Jap Zero fighters to use the .25s with tracer ammunition to make sure they were on target. When they saw the tracers disappearing into the target they would fire their two 20mm cannon. It was said that they did this to conserve the small number of cannon shells the Zeros carried. It was one of these shells that had perforated the right main fuel tank — why we never caught fire is still a mystery, but thank God we didn't.

'The next time we ran into difficulty was on 28 April 1944, during a strike mission to Wadke Island. I guess we were two hours or so into the flight over enemy territory when we noticed the left engine running rough. The next thing we knew, the cowling began to shred and the engine ground to a miserable halt. We had to get down and the nearest emergency landing place was a strip called Tadje which was in the process of being cleared by the Marines and other ground forces. They were still laying steel matting over the old Japanese airstrip and filling in the bomb holes — that we had made. I made contact with someone there through the assigned air-sea rescue frequency and was told that part of the strip was available for an emergency landing. We had two other options — fly out over the water and bail out or make a water landing with air sea rescue standing by.

'The consensus of opinion among the crew was that we'd take our gamble with the airstrip. This we did and landed successfully. But as the troops were still clearing out the Jap emplacements, with snipers still active, it was a kind of hairy situation. We felt kind of naked, not being equipped or trained to be in that kind of situation and were mighty glad to be led to a safe area where there was a foxhole to climb into.

'We learned later that our engine had apparently been hit by some kind of ground fire which had destroyed one of the cylinders by blowing the head clean off. Understandably, the engine chewed itself to pieces and took bits of the cowling with it.

'Mission No 49 was on 22 June 1944, when we flew to Ranski drome, Vokelkop. According to my log book we destroyed some aircraft and damaged the runway, duration of the mission being 5 hours, 15 minutes. After that I was scheduled to go back to the States.'

82
From New Guinea to Kyushu, the 'Sun Setters' fought a long, arduous war. The first full B-25 group in the 5th Air Force, its aircraft were decorated with suitably garish squadron insignia. Clockwise from the screaming eagle group badge, the sign board shows those of the Wolf Pack, Black Panthers, Tigers and Green Dragons. *Behrens*

82

Winged Arsenal

If there was one quality that all great military aircraft of WW2 possessed in abundance, it was adaptability. That quality translated into a variety of different attributes in different designs, but in armament, there were few types that could touch the extraordinary changes made between the early and late model B-25s. Field depots had shown what was possible to turn a docile medium bomber into a zero altitude killer and it remained only for North American to refine the aggressive potential in the last two production models.

On 31 July 1943, 43-4105, the prototype B-25H (NA-98) made its maiden flight with NAA Test pilot Robert J. Hilton at the controls. Essentially an interim bridge between the B-25G and J, the H set the standard for all succeeding examples. It was the first to feature a 'production' twin-gun tail position with seating and sighting cockpit for the gunner similar to many installations made on B-25C/D models, and introduced glazed waist windows as standard.

An improved Martin dorsal turret with a higher dome was re-positioned aft of the cockpit rather than the central fuselage location of earlier models and fixed forward-firing armament was standardised as eight .50-cal Browning M-2 machine guns, plus a lighter T-13E1 75mm cannon in the port side tunnel similar to that of the B-25G. Cannon weight was reduced in the B-25H to 775lb, compared to 1,445lb for the weapon fitted to most G models. Crew complement was five: pilot, navigator/radio operator/cannoneer, flight engineer/dorsal turret gunner, waist gunner/camera operator, and tail gunner.

83
Many refinements, including an improved 75mm cannon, went into the B-25H. The first of the deeper rear fuselage models with a twin-gun tail position, the H model had a relocated dorsal turret, four nose guns and invididual 'package' fairings for the side guns. In this view, an NAA plant technician is installing the ammunition tracks for the nose guns. The aircraft shown is in fact a PBJ-1H. *NAA*

83

84

84

One Man Operation: Cockpit view of the B-25H illustrates well the amount of firepower literally under the pilot's fingers. On the column cross bars, reading clockwise were: nose and package guns firing button; bomb and torpedo release button and cannon firing button. Where the co-pilot's feet rested in other models, there was a radio compass unit, with a flexible de-froster tube running forward on the left side. *NAA*

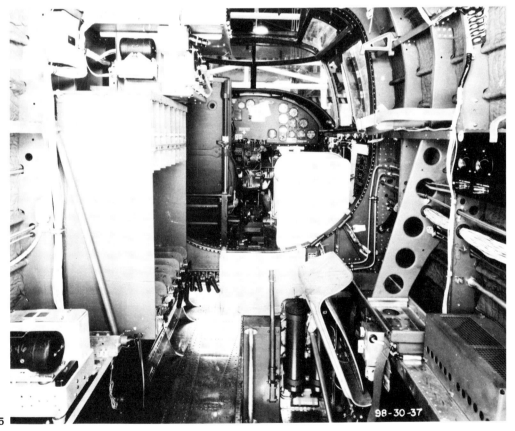

85

85

Moving backwards through the B-25H, past the navigator's riding seat to the right of the pilot and the ⅜in armour plate panel secured directly behind it on the bulkhead, you entered the compartment occupied by the navigator/cannoneer. On the left side is the armoured cannon shell rack, with a folded seat opposite. *NAA*

With B-25H production underway at Inglewood (1,000 examples were built in H-1, H-5 and H-10 blocks) Kansas City meanwhile prepared to phase in the B-25J (NA-108) which reverted to a glass nose with accommodation for a bombardier or an interchangeable solid strafer nose with eight machine guns. USAAF acceptance of the first B-25J was in December 1943 and until August 1945, 4,318 were built in eight sub-variants: B-25J-1; -5, -10, -15; -20; -25; -30 and -35.

Many detail changes were made during the course of J model production, although

86
The well-shielded gunner's position in the extreme tail of the B-25H was described in the manual as a turret — a Bell Model M-7 electro-hydraulic turret to be precise — although of course only the guns actually moved. Each weapon had 600 rounds and had a maximum elevation of 40 degrees upwards and 35 degrees downwards from the horizontal and extreme azimuth travel of 38 degrees each side of the aircraft's centre-line. The gun control handles, with integral firing buttons and interphone switches, can be seen on the top of the control column.
NAA

87
The side defence of the H model was also much improved by the larger gun hatches with their 'bay window' curved glass and socket (rather than post) mounted .50-cal guns. This view, looking towards the tail, shows the ammuntion feed from horizontal wall-mounted boxes aft of the two $\frac{1}{4}$in thick vertical armour plate section.
NAA

88
Ultimate Strafer: North American's beautifully streamlined solid nose section with eight .50-cal machine guns installed on a production J model. A cleaned up version of the old bombardier's 'greenhouse' section overpainted and filled with guns, this custom nose was compatible with earlier models as well as the J. *NAA*

89
Double Stinger: The business end of the H model with the canvas dust cover removed. *NAA*

90
Alternatively, you could order the medium bomber version with space for the bomb aimer and his equipment. Only marginally less firepower was provided in basic J model form (one flexible and one fixed .50-cal) although combat units added extra guns — or removed them as required. *NAA*

90

91
Tail Scan: The camera shows almost the entire visual area of the J model gunner's position. *NAA*

91

there was commonality between all variants 'off the line', irrespective of field modifications. This included: bombardier and bomb door controls duplicated in the pilot's cockpit; accommodation for a six-man crew; provision for three instead of two 1,000lb bombs or two 1,600lb armour-piercing bombs (maximum internal bomb size being limited to 2,000lb for a normal maximum bomb load of 4,000lb); and wing rack provision for up to six 325lb depth charges. The capability to carry an external torpedo was also retained throughout J production, although provision for aerial mines and glide bombs was introduced only from the 4,292nd aircraft, during the J-35 block.

The solid nose section was introduced on the B-25J-15 (from serial No 44-28711; 400 aircraft) and was subsequently fitted to 800 production aircraft, although field kits were made available to adapt in-service C/D aircraft. Armour plate was provided for the bombardier, pilot and co-pilot, side and tail gun positions and as protection from head-on attack in all models, the pilots and co-pilots seats being armour-plated from the B-25J-25; armour plate deflectors and fairings for the upper turret were introduced on the 2,686th machine.

Self-sealing wing fuel tanks held 970gal and a fuselage tank an additional 335gal. A 215gal bomb bay tank could be fitted depending on mission requirements, average range (with 4,000gal payload at an average 181kts) being 1,316 nautical miles. Combat speed was 245kts maximum power at 10,000ft, maximum speed 255kts at 15,000ft, normal power settings.

B-25Js were powered by Wright R-2600-13 or -29 engines giving respect-ively 2,600 or 2,800rpm for take off. Loadings were 19,530lb empty, 27,400lb combat weight (basic radius mission) with a maximum (take off and landing) weight of 35,000lb. The basic radius formula from which the preceeding figures were calculated envisaged a typical low altitude attack mission as: (1) a 10-minute normal rated power warm up and take off; (2) climb to 10,000ft, normal rated power; (3) cruise at long range speed to a point 30 minutes prior to target; (4) descend to sea level (no distance allowed); (5) cruise at long range speeds for 15 minutes followed by 15 minutes normal rated power bomb runs; (6) drop bombs and conduct five minutes evasive action at normal rated power (no distance gained); (7) make 10 minutes' normal rated power run out from target and climb to 10,000ft; (8) cruise back to base at long range speeds; and (9) land with 5% of initial fuel load as reserves. Radius of action for a high altitude bomb drop was rated similarly except that (4) was climb to reach 20,000ft 30 minutes prior to bomb drop and (7) make 10-minute normal rated power run out from target and descend to 10,000ft.

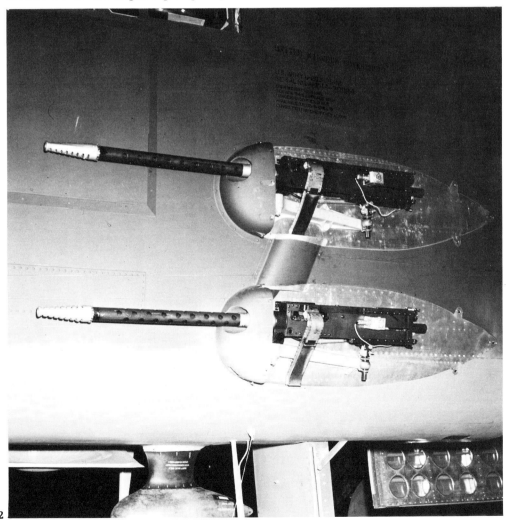

92

92
Interesting detail view of the side guns fitted to B-25J 44-29984 shows how the ammunition feed for the top weapon on each side required an external trunking section linking each blister. The barrels are fitted with flash-suppressors and the aircraft bears the wording 'United Kingdom Government' above the AAF data block stencilling. *NAA*

Spread Thin

At the end of February 1942, with the Japanese in possession of nearly all of South-East Asia, part of the remnants of Far East Air Force arrived in India — where the 10th Air Force was activated at Karachi on 12 February. The B-25 came to India in May, in the hands of the 11th Bomb Squadron.

The 11th's sojourn was brief as it quickly transferred to China to operate with the 14th Air Force, leaving the 22nd Squadron as the sole US medium bomber outfit on the sub continent. Further calls on its already meagre strength by other theatres reduced still further the number of aircraft available to the 10th, with the result that medium and heavy bombers operated together as the 7th Group for an interim period. By September there were more tangible signs of growth and the 341st Bomb Group was activated at Karachi on the 15th. The group had the

11th and 22nd Squadrons assigned, although the former remained in China, and two new squadrons, the 490th and 491st, were activated that same day to give a technical strength of four squadrons. In reality, both new units lacked aircraft and were little more than paper organisations for the time being.

To control forthcoming AAF and RAF operations in India, India Air Task Force was brought into being on 3 October, Brig-Gen Caleb V. Haynes commanding. Its primary tasks were defence of the Assam terminus of the Himalayan air ferry route and protection of the aircraft operatng the service.

Already masters of southern Burma, the Japanese moved to secure the northern areas in the autumn of 1942. The B-25 made its combat debut on 19 September and in the closing months of the year, the 22nd BS flew a further few missions with

93
The dispersed squadrons of the 341st Bomb Group operated deep into two of the world's largest land masses — northern India and China — throughout the war, under particularly harsh conditions for most of the time. This B-25C in typically beat up finish bears the unofficial eagle over mountains badge of the 22nd Squadron below the cockpit. *NAA*

93

95

These photographs show
crews of the 22nd BS with yet
another variation of
field-modified nose armament
on C/D models. Each aircraft
has four fixed guns, that on the
top left side being fitted with a
blast tube barrel extension.
Gen Claire Chennault, famed
commander of the Flying
Tigers and the 14th Air Force,
put on a suitably determined
expression for the crew
photograph above, while the
lettered sign held by crew
members of aircraft No 21 is
self-explanatory. The
rock-strewn dispersal is
noteworthy, as are the frag
bomb clusters below the
Mitchell's bomb bay. *NAA*

the 15 aircraft it then had on strength. On
the 25th, four B-25Cs attacked Hanoi and
placed several bombs on the runway of Gia
Lam airfield.

In the new year, the 491st and 490th
Squadrons flew their first missions, both
units sending aircraft against railway
targets — which were to occupy 10th AF
mediums for the rest of the war in Burma.
The 490th Squadron took the name 'Burma
Bridge Busters' for its intensive effort
against that particular form of transportation, although it frequently hit other types

of target, including airfields, river traffic
and road transport.

Sortie rate and bomb tonnage gradually
rose during 1943, with new fighter groups
bringing P-51 and P-38s into the 10th to
support the bombers — which as well as
more conventional loads, used mines to
sink river craft. The 341st, initially operating with B-25C/D models, received a
number of B-25G strafers to help soften up
well defended targets.

In November 1943, B-25s were assigned
to a large force of US and RAF aircraft

96
Burma Commandos: A section
of 1st Air Commando Group
B-25Hs in their distinctive
white stripe markings. Nearest
the camera is 43-4329, with
43-4360 in the lead and
43-4278 out to starboard.
USAF

97
Eastern 'Quaker. The 12th
Bomb Group brought
much-needed B-25 punch to
the CBI when it transferred
from the MTO in 1944. This H
model was *Prop Wash*, with
seven missions recorded at the
time of the photograph.
Howard Levy

attacking Rangoon. The 490th Squadron
supported the main strike by bombing
Mingaladon airfield on the 25th, escorted
by P-51As. Having dropped their bombs,
the Mitchells came under attack by Oscars
and Nicks — which met strong resistance
from defensive guns. One enemy fighter
was claimed destroyed, plus three pro-
bables and two damaged.

As 1944 opened, the 10th received
reinforcements in the shape of new groups

released from action in other theatres.
From the Mediterranean came the 12th
Bomb Group, equipped mainly with new
B-25H and J models, its 81st and 82nd
Squadrons occupying Tezgaon and the
83rd and 434th Kurmitola during March.
Declared operational in the new theatre
the following month, the Earthquakers
went on to build on an already impressive
record.

Mining sorties, using two US Mk 13 or

British Mk V mines, continued to be a part of the 10th AF's medium bomber missions; it was found that the best delivery technique was individual release in bright moonlight conditions, each aircraft flying at between 300 to 500ft altitude.

Early in the year, British forces had begun the second Arakan campaign to forestall a Japanese invasion of India. Temporarily checked by a surrounded but well air-supplied force at Chittagong, the Japanese faced further setbacks when Orde Wingate's Chindits were landed behind their lines.

To provide support for Wingate's special force, the 5318th Air Unit was activated in India. Occupying bases at Lalaghat and Hailakandi, the unit, which had a dozen B-25Hs comprising a medium bomber element, went into action on 12 February, when B-25s bombed railway bridges at Meya and Kani.

B-25s also flew reconnaissance missions in the vicinity of Wingate's two proposed jungle landing grounds, 'Piccadilly' and 'Broadway'. On 5 March, gliders went into the latter, Piccadilly having been discovered and blocked by the enemy. Close

co-operation between the B-25s and 5318th P-51s ensured the success of a well planned operation and kept the Japanese covered in the air and on the ground. Between them, the Mitchells and Mustangs dealt with any target: the fighters carried guns, bombs and rockets, the B-25s guns, bombs and heavy calibre cannon. Losses were light considering the high sortie rate before and after Wingate's forces went in.

Five days before the 5318th officially became the 1st Air Commando Group, Orde Wingate was killed. On 24 March he accepted a lift in the aircraft flown by Lt Brian Hodges. The B-25 took off from Imphal and headed for Wingate's headquarters, then located at Sylhet on the other side of the Naga Hills, which separate Burma from Assam. The last sighting of the Mitchell was some six minutes before it crashed in the hills, killing all aboard.

'Working on the railroads' continued to be the specialist activity of 10th Air Force mediums throughout the spring and summer of 1944; interspersed with strikes on supply dumps and bridge structures, the B-25 crews polished the task of keeping the

98
Commanders: Gen George E. Stratemeyer, Commanding General, AAF China Theatre, who officially took over from Chennault as head of the Army Air Forces in China on 6 July 1945 (left) with Col Lewis B. Wilson, 12th Group CO from September 1945 and Major Thompson, 81st Bomb Squadron CO (right) during a visit to the 'Earthquakers' base at Fenny, India.
Howard Levy

99
Flypast: Men of the 12th attend Memorial Day services while two B-25s mark the occasion in appropriate fashion; Tezgoan, May 1944.
Howard Levy

100
Misfortunes of War: During his wartime service as an AAF photographer, Howard Levy recorded many facets of operational life, including the occasional 'crack up'. This and the following four photographs show one such in the sequence in which events occurred. It was the 19 August 1944 mission, the target for the 12th being Burmese railway yards. B-25H No 83 (believed to have been 43-4432) was fourth in line as the 434th Bomb Squadron taxied out past a solitary RAF Spitfire at Comilla, India.

lines disabled for long periods. Masters at quick repair of shattered tracks, the Japanese managed to keep their trains running, necessitating dangerous, repeat attacks to cut the lines again. While bombs could break rails easily enough, often in dozens of separate places, the enemy needed much more time to fill in holes in the roadbeds. The answer was the spike bomb which, unlike conventional bombs, would not ricochet off rails and sleepers. With the aid of a steel spike that could be screwed into the nose of a demolition bomb, the Earthquakers caused lasting damage. The group's 81st Squadron flew its first CBI mission on 16 April, and the first spike bomb sorties two days later. The recommended technique was to sow the bombs in pairs at half-mile intervals with the aircraft flying at 220mph; on its first spike bomb mission, the 81st dropped 144 along the Sagaing-Shwebo line and scored 25 direct hits. Numerous subsequent sorties caused widespread destruction, particularly when large bombs were fitted with spikes.

By the end of April 1944, the 12th's other three squadrons had flown their first missions and on 17 May, the group's aircraft made a spectacular attack on the Chauk petroleum plant, causing fires that sent smoke up to 10,000ft. As part of the 3rd Tactical Air Force, the group continued to pound Japanese targets, particularly those at Myitkyina, Burma, until it fell to Allied force in August.

The 490th Squadron's war of the rails went on until 1945, being awarded a DUC for a particular effort in the last three months of 1944. In December 1944, the 12th Group had moved to Fenny in India, where it remained until moving to Meiktila (81st and 82nd) and Magwe (83rd and 434th) in Burma during the spring of 1945. The 490th BS left Moran, India for Warazup. Burma, in November 1944, where it remained until departing for China in April 1945. Although the 1st Air Commando Group relinquished its B-25 element during a temporary withdrawal from combat in May 1944, its Mitchells are believed to have remained in India, under its control, until at least early 1945.

While the exploits of the modestly-sized CBI air forces never received the publicity afforded combat groups in other more accessible theatres, North American Aviation kept its workers informed of the deeds of B-25 crews around the world via the columns of the company magazine *Skyline*. Combat vignettes, accompanied by suitably dramatic artwork, helped show the soundness of the aircraft the firm was building. This was one such concerning the 10th Air Force:

'One of the most remarkable flying feats in

101
Some, including No 82, 43-4217, made it safely.

102
But No 83 didn't make it and wound up in the rice paddy at the end of the runway — the right landing gear had given way and there was a flash of flame before impact. Luckily, the crew got out with only 'minor damage'.

103
A bit later there was a massive 'boom' when seven out of eight 500lb Composition (special strength) B-bombs went off, taking No 83 with them. Meanwhile, the mission went on and a successful strike was made. Picking his way through the debris was the Ordnance Officer, en route to remove the fuse from the remaining unexploded bomb. He only happened to be standing nearby, checking the take-off and was surprised by the accident. Howard himself got a bit wet and had to dodge falling bits when the sky lit up.

101

102

103

the CBI was accomplished by the late Lt William E. Cook, of Fullerton, California. After a successful bridge-busting mission deep in Burma for the 10th AF's Eastern Air Command, the Mitchell that Cook was flying ran into an area of intense ack-ack. Cook threw the ship into evasive action and hit the deck to escape the enemy's fire. He had flown clear of the danger, when he ran into a church spire. The impact sheared off four feet of the left wing of his B-25 and wrenched loose several feet of aileron. Home base was several hundred miles away, and the men were shaken by their harrowing mission. But the young lieutenant was a brilliant pilot and had

104

faith in a tough airplane. Flying literally on a wing and a prayer, he brought the crew home to safety.'

Although American Army Air Forces, China, Burma and India had been established at Chungking under Gen Stillwell as early as 4 March 1942, it was to be some six weeks after the Doolittle raid before B-25s again flew over China on a combat mission. On 3 June six B-25Cs from the 11th BS took off from Dinjam, India to strike Lashio airfield in Burma before flying on to Kunming. Scattered by bad weather, the force nevertheless bombed the target and shook off an enemy fighter attack in the process. Flying north at 10,000ft through a solid overcast, three aircraft crashed into mountains; a fourth ran out of fuel after becoming lost although the crew bailed out and were able to rejoin their unit about two weeks later. But the loss of four aircraft and three crews under-lined the hazards to be faced over the vast, sparsely populated and often hostile terrain of China.

Seven Tokyo raiders were in the crews of the next six 11th BS B-25s that arrived at Kunming, as the majority of Doolittle's small force was still in China at that time. On 4 July, the 11th and the 23rd Fighter Group became the vanguard of the China Air Task Force, created as a matter of

104
The offending gear leg was found and examined by interested parties, including the 12th's Maintenance Officer (centre) an RAF officer (left) and a second AAF officer.

105
By November 1944, the 12th had numerous J models in addition to its faithful Hs. Two Js, 43-3882/22 and 43-3901/23 accompany B-25H 43-4262/14 in this November 1944 shot of an 81st Squadron element. The faded finish of all three as well as the 'blotched' areas of paint on No 14 was indicative of the climate and the operational conditions. *Howard Levy*

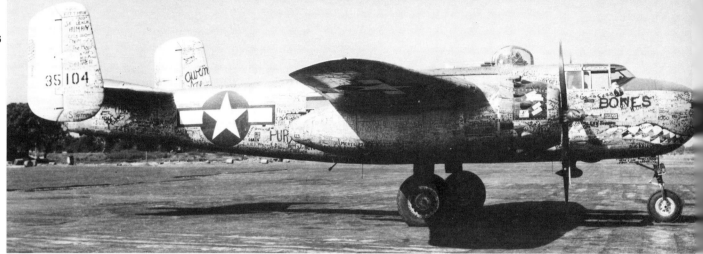

106
Signed off: The thousandth B-25H was the famous *Bones* which went to war covered in the signiatures of the workers at Inglewood. Actually the 3,208th Mitchell completed at the California plant before it went over exclusively to building Mustangs, '104 received approval for its final 'finish' from none other than Gen Hap Arnold. It was officially presented to Brig-Gen Donald H. Stace, chief of the western procurement district of the AAF on 7 July 1944 by NAA President Dutch Kindelberger. Ferried to the 3rd AF at Hunter Field, Georgia, 'Bones' arrived in India on 30 November 1944. Assigned to the 82nd BS, the aircraft took tail number 45 and flew its first mission on 6 December, to a bridge near Toungoo, Burma.
Howard Levy

107
In the meantime, the 490th Bomb Squadron was also building a fine reputation attacking Burmese bridge targets. This B-25C 42-32263 shows typical squadron markings and armament modifications, the squadron's 'flying skull' insignia being widely applied. (The aircraft in the background is an RAF Avro Anson Mk I.) *via R. L. Ward*

108
What Goes Down . . . occasionally comes back up! 'Earthquaker' personnel pluck out a bomb fuse that bounced when one of the B-25Hs went in low over the target.
Howard Levy

necessity by 10th Air Force. For months the 11th's Mitchells were the only bombers available to raid Japanese installations in a period marked by a lack of most items critical to even a limited air offensive. Tired and hungry men could still fly missions in patched up aircraft awaiting proper overhaul and spares — but they could not fly without fuel. And every drop the 14th Air Force used had to be hauled in from India over the Himalayan mountains, the notorious 'hump route' that held many dangers, of which enemy fighter attacks were sometimes the lesser.

CATE bombers were under the command of Col Caleb V. Haynes; he led the 15 July mission to the docks at Hankow and the major, 12-ship strike on Hong Kong on 25 October by which time he was CO of the India Air Task Force, and a Brigadier-General. Made up of elements of B-25s from the 11th and 22nd Squadrons, the latter raid was a great success despite the loss of one Mitchell, the force causing damage in the city's dock and warehousing area and the Kowloon ferry terminal. A second raid on Hong Kong took place on the night of the 12th/13th, six B-25s bombing the city while three others went after warehouses at Canton.

On 10 March 1943, the 14th AF was activated at Kunming and absorbed CATF under the command of Gen Claire L. Chennault. By then, the 11th BS had become part of the 341st Group, although the unit operated in China virtually independently until 1944.

In common with the majority of B-25C and D models in US service, the 11th's aircraft were modified to suit them better to combat requirements. The ventral turret was removed and replaced by two down and rearwards-firing hand held machine guns, all early missions calling for conventional medium altitude bombing, for which some form of underside protection against fighter attack was deemed necessary. When Chennault designated Japanese held ports and shipping as primary targets for his mediums from 1 July 1943, some of the 11th's bombardier-nose Mitchells were rigged as strafers, the unit also using the B-25H.

Lend-Lease arrangements had also ensured that the B-25 would be included in the total of more than 1,350 aircraft the Chinese Air Force would receive as new equipment; 131 B-25s were eventually delivered, at least three (C, H and J) of the main production models flying in Nationalist colours. Chinese B-25Cs also had their lower turrets removed, as recalled by Constantine L. Zakhartchenko, Senior Aeronautical Engineer and Technical Advisor for the Bureau of Aeronautical Research of the Commission on Aeronautical Affairs of China:

'When the first Mitchell bombers arrived in China, it was soon obvious that the bottom turret was useless and that the Japanese were aware of the rear blind spot as well as of the absence of forward firing armament, and they used that knowledge advantageously. Colonel Caleb Haynes got hold of me and I, on my own, went ahead on the basis of Chiang's order (to provide full co-operation and satisfy any demands of the American forces) without waiting for the Commission's approval. At the First Aircraft Factory, we revised B-25 armament by installing two .50 calibre guns from the bottom turret alongside the bombsight in the nose, and replacing the bottom turret by two manually-operated .30 cal guns. Additionally, we installed a remotely-controlled .30cal tail gun on a saxaphone mount which produced a random cone of tracer bullets and was very effective in keeping enemy fighters away.

'Col Haynes was delighted and requested seven sets of blueprints for Washington. We were very short of blueprint paper and I stipulated that they must get us replacement paper from India, which was agreed to, but the paper never arrived. In the meantime, I had to justify to the Commission the spending of several thousand man-hours of engineering and labour. I asked for the photographs of the installations to attach to my report to the Commission. The photos were promised, but a few days after the Executive Officer of the bombardment group arrived and sheepishly confessed that the regulations did not permit photography of US aircraft armament.

'On my way back to the US, I noticed while crossing Africa that new B-25s going east continued to be equipped with bottom turrets, in spite of our report — of several

109

109
Working along a river bank which obviously yielded a prime target, an 82nd Squadron B-25H turns away for another pass or the run back to its East Bengal base. *Howard Levy*

110
Nos 29 and 25 (43-4907) approaching base over flat scrubland, their war having but a few months to run. *Howard Levy*

months previously — of their complete uselessness. When I asked in Washington I was told that the consideration of revision and contract changes requires time.'

The Chinese American Combat Wing went operational in October 1943 and provided much-needed muscle to the medium bomber effect in the CBI. The CACW had a 1st Bomb Group with four squadrons of B-25s, their Chinese pilots having received training under Lend-Lease. American and Chinese officers acted as group, squadron and flight commanders.

Chennault's anti-shipping campaign opened for the B-25 on 27 July, when the 11th BS sent six aircraft against a transport sighted off Stonecutter Island. And although the emphasis had shifted to potentially more profitable targets for the mediums, it was not before the closing months of 1943 that the 14th was able to overcome enforced groundings, often for weeks on end, due to lack of essential supplies.

As the supply situation improved and more aircraft arrived in China, the 14th was able to send its bombers and fighters against a wide variety of targets including aerodromes, troop concentrations, storage areas, rail yards and ammunition dumps. The first 'sea sweep' by B-25s was on 27 September, the mediums ranging out from Nanning into the Gulf of Tonkin. In October there were 15 missions, mainly against shipping, for the loss of three B-25s.

A spectacular surprise attack was made on 25 November when 14 Mitchells hit Shinchiku airfield on Formosa, escorted by P-51s and P-38s. In a perfectly timed single pass across the field, the US force destroyed about 22 Japanese aircraft for no losses to its own. Skip bombing and strafing attacks on shipping netted the 11th Squadron a total of 39 vessels during 1943 — 48,900 tons; 19 vessels were damaged and one destroyer and a gunboat were also sunk. By the end of the year, the squadron had 23 B-25s on hand.

Late in 1943, steps were taken to rationalise the 14th AF chain of command with the result that the 11th BS joined the 23rd FG as part of the 68th Composite Wing at Kweilin, the wing HQ being responsible for all air combat units operating east of longitude 108E and including the CACW squadrons. The 69th CW, with jurisdiction over units based west of that longitude, had the 341st Bomb Group, which officially became part of the 14th AF in January 1944, and the 51st Fighter Group. In practice, the 341st Group had only two under-strength squadrons the 22nd and 491st. The 490th BS remained on attachment to the 10th AF and the 11th continued to operate independently for the time being.

For the 14th's mediums, the first quarter of 1944 was a period of careful fuel conservation and single aircraft missions often without fighter escort. Such missions were occasionally highly effective if surprise

was achieved. From the start of CBI operations, medium bombers also flew as part of a combined force of heavies and fighters — the latter often acting as fighter bombers — to strike a particular target with the maximum available strength.

But just as in other areas, the lightning, 'hit and run' low level strike remained the Mitchell's forte; on 4 March 1944, one such attack achieved good results. Six 11th Squadron aircraft surprised Kiungshan airfield on the northern tip of Hainan Island. Roaring in under the enemy's radar they blasted the hard-standings and installations with guns and frag clusters. It was all over in less than 60 seconds, the B-25s' single line abreast pass leaving more than 20 Japanese aircraft in flames.

In the meantime, the ground situation in China was not going well. On 17 April the Japanese began a series of offensives aimed at opening a north-south corridor from the Yellow River to Hankow and southwards to the Indo China border. The enemy's intention was to secure a railway link between northern China and Indo China — and to isolate 14th Air Force bases. On the 19th, two Japanese divisions drove south and a second force struck northwards to meet it along the 240-mile length of the Peiping-Hankow railway. The CACW hammered these movements, attacking river traffic, airfields, staging areas and bridges over the Yellow River. With only 11 medium bombers and 31 fighters, the wing made a supreme effort,

stopped the US air base at Sian from being overrun and won a DUC in the process.

Supporting a Chinese counter offensive in May, the 22nd BS was heavily committed on the Salween River front, the objective being to open a land supply route from Assam to Kunming. This particularly gruelling offensive was to last until the end of the year, when the Chinese had taken Tengchung, the Sung Shan strongpoint on the Burma Road and finally, Langling and Mangshih.

By mid-1944 more fighters and transports had arrived in China to boost the 14th, although the ground situation was anything but stable. Advancing Japanese troops captured Hengyang airfield on 26 June, the first 14th AF base to be lost. Fighters were heavily engaged in trying to stop the advance and medium bombers were out over the city itself early in July. The Chinese succeeded in temporarily halting the invaders, but bad weather reduced the number of support sorties the 14th could fly, and after holding out for 42 days, the city of Hengyang capitulated. Throughout the battle, B-25s of the 11th, 491st and 4th Bomb Squadrons, the latter from the CACW, made repeated attacks on trucks, bridges, aircraft and river craft.

More friendly air bases were threatened by the second Japanese attack of 1944, which steam-rollered down the Hankow-Hanoi railway towards Kweilin and Luichow. Ling-ling had been lost by

111
Although the Air Commandos relinquished their medium bomber element in May 1944 a number of 'candy striped' machines were still in India as late as January 1945. These B-25Hs were on the line at Chittagong at that time. *USAF*

8 September and in the next two months or so, five other bases — Henygang, Kweilin, Linchow, Tanchuk and Nanning, fell into enemy hands. The culmination of the eight month campaign was the link-up of Japanese forces in Indo China and the establishment of a transportation route northwards as far as Peiping. Even worse for the 14th, the new enemy gains threatened Kweiyang, Kunming and even Chunking.

Throughout this critical period, AAF bomber and fighter groups maintained what pressure they could across the vast land areas being overrun by the Japanese armies, as well as mounting sorties on strategic targets. Hong Kong was subject to a night raid by a typical mixed formation on 16 October, when eight B-25s, in company with B-24s under Lightning and Mustang escort, went in at low level. A successful strike rounded off with the mediums sinking 28,000 tons of shipping in Victoria harbour.

By November the medium bomber force available to the 14th AF had risen to 109 B-25s out of a total for all types of over 700. And as 1944 drew to a close, the 68th CW was engaged mainly in support of the Chinese Army in the south and southeast while the 69th Wing operated over southwest China, northern Burma and Indo China and provided protection for the Hump ferry route. In central China, the CACW was occupied south of the Yellow River.

Although early 1945 was marked by fresh Chinese offensives to recapture lost territory, it was not until 4 February that Kunming was liberated. By that time the land route to China from Burma had been opened — for the first time since 1942 — China did not have to rely solely on air supply to sustain her war effort.

Having secured the remaining links in the Hankow-Canton railway by the end of January, the Japanese moved against the 14th AF's eastern bases. They had taken Suichwan, Namyung and Kanchow by early February, leaving only Changting in that part of the country.

In the south, the 341st's B-25s were doing their best to prevent enemy supply movements by rail. Mindful of the ever-present difficulties in attacking bridges, the group devised 'glip bombing' whereby attacking aircraft adopted three rapid changes of altitude to distract enemy gunners in the target area. Bridges were invariably well defended and the bomb run often had to be made through narrow valleys and gorges. Even so, the 341st succeeded in reducing its tonnage per bridge destroyed to 7.75, a remarkably economical achievement.

Despite their hopeless situation elsewhere the Japanese were still making gains in China as late as March 1945, during which month they captured Laohokow airfield. It was to be the last 14th AF base to fall, as henceforward, Chinese resistence stiffened. Further enemy advances were held until 8 April, when the final Japanese offensive began. Driving west into Hunan Province, which contained Chinchiang airfield, the enemy put 60,000 troops into the field on an 80-mile front. But with the Chinese armies swelled to 100,000 men, the Japanese were forced to slow down and stop after about 25 miles. They began to fall back, pursued by the Chinese until by 7 June, all lost territory was again in friendly hands. Ranging over the vast battlefields, American and Chinese bomber and fighter crews gave admirable support, so much so that the outcome was never again in doubt.

112
With a backdrop of Mustangs, this unarmed B-25J of the Chinese Air Force was at Kangwan airfield circa 1945/46. Flown with distinction by Nationalist crews, B-25s of the Chinese-American Composite Wing fought the Japanese until virtually the last day of World War 2.
Earl Reinert via Ernie McDowell

112

Tough Underbelly

As a prelude to the assault on Italy, Allied airpower sought to isolate the invasion area by cutting all possible supply lines to German forces in the south and prevent Luftwaffe interference with the landings. Of primary importance was the Italian railway system, representing a series of targets requiring attention until the last days of the war. With Italy having signed an armistice before the first landing craft grounded on the beaches of Salerno, the German cause in the Mediterranean suffered a severe blow and the Luftwaffe fighter force could do little to hamper the invasion. Aerial opposition was extremely light although as usual, German flak was a hazard to air operations.

Many thousands of sorties were made by fighters, dive bombers, heavies and mediums as the US 5th and British 8th Armies linked up on 16 September to secure the entire lower 'boot' of Italy. During the month, all B-25 groups had flown 3,394 sorties, lost 17 aircraft and had two reported missing. Damage had been sustained by 61 aircraft, the sortie rate achieved by B-25s being exceeded only by the P-38 groups.

With winter approaching, the 340th established its first Italian base at San Pancrazio from 17 October, the 321st having taken over Grottaglie on the 3rd. The following month would see the 12th Group based at Foggia.

Ground forces began meeting stiff opposition at the Gustav Line during October and November, at the start of more than six months' bitter fighting before Allied troops liberated Rome. From 1 January, Lt-Gen Ira C. Eaker took over command of Mediterranean Allied Air Forces and Maj-Gen John K. Cannon became Commanding General of the 12th AF on the 26th.

On 14 January, the 340th's 486th Squadron drew the railway bridge and marshalling yards at Pontecorvo as its target. Nine B-25s were despatched from Pompeii at 1315 hours, the formation being commanded by Major Lou Keller. Flak was described as heavy, accurate and intense as the B-25s ran into the target. One Mitchell went down over the bridge with a wing shot away. Maj Keller's aircraft was

113

113
Bowing out: After 66 missions, *Shanghi Lil* a B-25C of the 310th Bomb Group, returned to the US in the hands of Capt J. H. Beatty and his crew, all of whom seem happy to comply with that particular order. *USAF*

114
Monastic Mission: The might of the 340th Group's 488th Squadron drones towards Cassino, 15 March 1944. Renowned throughout the Mediterranean theatre for its bombing accuracy, the group overcame a number of setbacks and was the pride of the 57th Bomb Wing, the famed 'Bridge Busters'. *USAF*

115
Nature's Flak: Two days after the 15 March mission, Mount Vesuvius erupted and caused havoc amongst dispersed 340th Group B-25s on Pompeii airfield. Hot ash and rocks smashed plexiglass, melted tyres and burned fabric off control surfaces. Little could be done for about 80 Mitchells, as this 23 March photo graphically shows. Vesuvius still glowers in the background. *USAF via NAA*

badly shot up and limped back across the bomb line, where the entire crew bailed out. It was Maj Keller's third jump from a crippled B-25:

'As soon as we had dropped the last 1,000lb bomb, we received a near miss which wounded the pilot, Lt Swope, and also myself, riding co-pilot. The flak burst hit the left engine, causing the prop to run away. As Lt Swope's left arm had been hit, I was flying the ship. Lt Swope immediately feathered the right engine. We then made a right turn to get back into friendly territory, trying to do evasive action. It was about this time that we received more near misses, damaging the left engine. I noticed that the left engine's oil pressure was fluctuating seriously but as this was the last engine, we coaxed the ship across the bomb line, at which time I ordered everyone to abandon ship.

'Just as Lt Swope had left the ship, the port engine ran away and I feathered the prop. I then realised how quiet it was with no engines, but time was wasting. I made two turns, one to the right, one to the left. I then looked at my altimeter, air speed and rate of climb instruments. My altitude was about 5,000ft, my air speed 185mph and my rate of descent about 1,500ft per minute. I decided to jump.

'I moved over to the pilot's seat as it was pushed back, but I couldn't get it forward. I scrambled between the seats after carefully trimming the airplane and jumped into the broad open spaces. Finnito.'

Major Keller survived the descent and landed on the right side of the bomb line. Not so T/Sgt Moran, radioman/gunner of another B-25, who had taken to his 'chute after the aircraft's interphone went out and had one engine stopped and on fire. Moran landed in enemy territory. His understandably rapid exit was nevertheless too hasty, as the pilot, 2-Lt D. E. Glade, succeeded in bringing the crippled bomber and the rest of the crew safely home.

A fourth B-25 also suffered from the attentions of the Pontecorvo flak: pilot 2-Lt C. J. Clark, despite being blinded by flying glass, landed safely at Pomigliano. Seven men were lost on the raid and five injured, none seriously, in damaged aircraft. Two B-25s failed to return and all nine were holed by flak.

If Pompeii had an ominous ring to those versed in ancient history, the proximity of Vesuvius caused the 340th little concern — not that is, until March. Earlier, someone had suggested dropping a bomb into the crater just to see if the volcano would erupt, but it soon became obvious that such a manifestation required no human help. Although the volcano had been dormant for 38 years, it had rumbled for weeks, belching forth great clouds of smoke and white vapour during the day and at night creating a red glow to help guide the bombers home. During the last week of March activity increased and on the night of the 17th/18th, Vesuvius blew. Awoken by earth tremors and explosions, airmen rushed from their quarters to witness the

117

sky alight with vast shooting red fingers of fire and huge globs of lava bubbling from the rim of the crater.

Helmets were hastily donned to ward off the showers of cinders and smoking clinkers as people streamed down from the lower slopes to take refuge from the tide of lava engulfing their villages. Pompeii airfield, nestled right against the volcano, was subjected to a rain of hot ash. Dawn showed the extent of the damage caused to the 340th's aircraft. Every B-25 on the field — the group was well up to strength with about 80 aircraft — stood in a carpet of ash up to the top of its wheels. There were gaping holes in ailerons, rudders and elevators, the fabric covering burned away or hanging in tatters. Ground crews picked

over the wrecks but it was obvious that every bomber was beyond economical repair. The 340th had little choice but to pack what remained of its equipment and evacuate. Other groups in the vicinity of Vesuvius had been luckier and were able to fly most of their aircraft out, but the 340th was temporarily out of business, grounded for the third time 'by natural causes'.

When it had new aircraft to fly, the group undertook a few more missions before moving to Corsica on 15 April. Established in spartan surroundings, the men soon organised collections to enhance basic Army rations and a B-25 was despatched to Sicily two or three times a month to provision with fresh vegetables and eggs. On one such trip, the buyer had successfully negotiated the purchase of nearly 2,000 eggs and a mess sergeant dutifully set about loading them into the tail of the B-25, using layers of straw as cushioning material. It was too much; delicately balanced at the best of times, the Mitchell rocked back on to its tail and the result was 'one mess of scrambled eggs'.

Provisioning flights held other hazards. One B-25, loaded up with club liquor, took off at nightfall, missed the tip of Sardinia en route to Corsica and landed on Majorca. The Spanish authorities released the unhappy crew, but impounded the aircraft. A few weeks later, the group was informed that the hooch was awaiting collection in Gibraltar. Apparently the Spaniards had sampled the stuff and packed it rapidly on its way to its rightful owners.

116, 117
The Morning After: Maintenance crews did the rounds all the same, but the repair task would have been next to impossible. Undaunted, the 340th borrowed aircraft and flew the next scheduled mission. *USAF via NAA*

Corsica being somewhat lacking as an entertainment centre meant that men were freely allowed three-day passes for Naples and later, Rome. These R and R trips worked out well unless the weather socked in and stranded people. Leonard Kaufman CO of the 489th Squadron recalls:

'I landed at Naples (Cappodechino) one day after such a weather period. I found a group of men ready to get back home (they had been there about 8-10 days and were broke, tired and ready to head back). I checked the airplane and found we had 12 parachutes on board, which meant we could take eight. We selected the eight who had been there the longest and told the rest that we could send another airplane for them. We loaded and took off. The airplane seemed sluggish on take off and after we became airborne, I turned around and looked back to the navigator's compartment — all I could see was heads. After a count, I found we had 17 men on board. For one I didn't know if I should be angry with them for disobeying an order or wonder if it was a compliment that they would fly with me without them all having parachutes.'

That incident highlights the ability of the B-25 to lift loads way above the manufacturer's maximum, yet still be very forgiving, an asset frequently called upon during the nomadic life some groups were forced to lead in the MTO. Moving to a new base could be accomplished far more quickly if the bombers could double as transports and equipment of all kinds was invariably crammed into every available space. Nevertheless, it had to be done carefully, bearing in mind the balance. The recommended procedure was to load the nose and bomb bay first, then start the engines to hold the nose down and finally fill up the rear fuselage.

Providing enough aircraft for missions from Corsica demanded much from the ground crews, as the island was definitely not top of the AAF list for delivery of spares and supplies. Any aircraft that cracked up was immediately cannibalised for useful parts and many non-regulation practices were condoned to meet mission requirements. Muscle power often proved faster than regulation equipment when it came to loading bombs. In lieu of cranes or winches they were heaved aboard by hand and in general, the quickest available method was used. This also applied to unloading, both from vehicles and aircraft when the need arose. Drivers of the $2\frac{1}{2}$ton 6×6 bomb trucks would be given a spot to unload, drop the tailgate, back up at full speed and slam on the brakes, allowing the bombs to unload themselves. Minimising the chore of changing bombs once they had been loaded was equally expedient. Once they had been de-fuzed, someone would hit the salvo switch and drop the lot. They would be dragged away as the new load, perhaps frag clusters or incendiaries, was made ready. Occasionally this procedure caused

118
En route to an Italian target, a waist gunner photographed part of a 447th BS formation, including a B-25J-5 and a D-30 (43-3522). The 321st Group dropped the Roman numeral squadron identifiers in favour of Arabic numerals during the winter of 1944-45.
USAF

118

near-panic to base visitors. Leo Kaufman once agreed to take two Service Command officers back to Naples in a B-25 that had been on standby for that day's mission, and it was still loaded with 1,000 pounders. Standing under the wing, the CO explained to his passengers that there would be a short delay while the unwanted bombs were removed. At that moment there was a multiple thump as the four bombs hit the ground. Kaufman had to grab the officers to keep them from 'running to the hills'.

With the 12th Group having departed the MTO in April, the spring of 1944 saw the three B-25 groups distributed thus: the 310th had its 379th, 380th, 381st and 428th Squadrons at Fano; the 321st had two squadrons, the 445th and 446th at Solenzara on Corsica with the 447th and 448th at Gaudo in Italy and the 340th was at Alesan, Corsica, in its entirety. Thus the B-25 squadrons, plus three groups of B-26s on Sardinia, one of A-20s in Italy and six groups of P-47s in both Italy and on Sardinia, plus two reconnaissance squadrons, one on Sardinia and one in Italy, were poised to execute Operation 'Strangle'. Designed to break the stalemate forced by German resistance at Cassino and the Anzio beachhead, Strangle was an all out interdiction of enemy supply lines, both on land and at sea. The mediums were heavily enaged, initially against rail traffic and between March and May the campaign achieved its first objective, the cutting of all rail routes to Rome.

German reaction was occasionally fierce and damaging if it surprised Allied aircraft on the ground, such as happened on 12 May. Again, it was the long-suffering 340th which was on the receiving end. Having re-equipped with new aircraft

after the Pompeii debacle the group was heavily attacked by Ju88s during the early hours of the morning. When it was over, the group counted 30 B-25s destroyed and another 45 badly damaged. In what was becoming a familiar ritual, the 340th salvaged what it could and went back into action, initially using borrowed aircraft. Seemingly thriving on adversity, it did not miss one day's operations and on 13 May provided 12 aircraft. New B-25s were delivered in time for Diadem, the offensive against the Gustav Line, the success of which enabled Allied troops to enter the Eternal City on 4 June.

Allied close air support was so effective that the Germans abandoned a planned defence of Rome and by late June their forces had been pushed northwards about 80 miles. Attention then focused on support for Operation 'Anvil', the invasion of southern France, the 12th's mediums dividing their efforts between support for the armies in Italy and striking communications and installations in France. Medium bombers were given the job of destroying all bridges on the Po River, which at that time had 23. Ten were assigned to the B-26s of the 42nd Bomb Wing and 13 to the 57th Wing's B-25s.

The air plan for 'Anvil' called for a concentrated 30-day assault on enemy airfields and lines of communication prior to the troops going ashore and thereafter engage in close support as the need arose. The build up of air units and supplies on Corsica proceeded through July and by early August MAAF had the entire 57th Wing and the A-20s of the 47th Group; US fighters and transports and RAF and French Air Force squadrons, a force totalling more than 2,100 aircraft on 14 airfields. But due to commitments in Italy, the

Taking in natural beauty that cannot be appreciated to the full, a crew of a 381st BS B-25J presses on, with 68 missions already 'on the board'. *USAF*

mediums did not begin 'Anvil' strikes until 2 August, when 57 B-25s attacked the Var River bridges; two days later the full weight of MAAF's carefully marshalled force was thrown against targets in southern France. Bad weather hampered operations on the 5th, but thereafter mediums, fighter bombers and heavies systematically reduced the railway and road system, B-25s and B-26s integrating their bombing to ensure that damage was not made good by the enemy. This was not always possible to achieve completely, but by D-day five of the six major bridges across the Rhone between Lyon and the coast were unuseable, the bombers' efforts being backed up by widespread action by French resistance groups, which cut rail lines in numerous places to completely disrupt enemy movement of troops and supplies.

The pre-invasion assault was greatly aided by the poor showing of the Luftwaffe; on the few occasions that enemy fighters did appear, they were rapidly dealt with by large numbers of Allied interceptors. Even so, the plan called for the bombing of airfields in three main areas from which the Germans might attack — Toulon, Udine and the Po Valley. There followed a bombardment of coastal gun batteries 24 hours before the invasion got underway on the morning of 15 August. And when the troops had gained a foothold, the mediums continued to contain the Germans behind the lines and isolate their forces from the invasion areas in the largest one day air effort in the Mediterranean to date.

As the troops forged inland, the mediums were tasked to participate in the limited but necessary series of sorties against airfields. Thus on D+5, 35 B-25s left their calling cards at Valence/Trésorerie although there was little more work of this nature to be done. So rapid was the advance that Allied commanders did not wish to have the bombers destroy airfields which friendly aircraft were soon to use themselves. The mediums returned to their main task of cutting lines of communication, particularly those across the Rhone and the Alps. This phase of the operation was left mainly to the 57th Wing's B-25s as the B-26s were occupied elsewhere. Nine bridges were consequently bombed between 17 and 20 August. All of them were damaged but only two, at Tussilage and Valence, knocked down. Nevertheless, this latest damage, added to that previously inflicted, left only one road bridge at Avignon open.

The bridge-busting mediums were then called off as the ground advance had been

so rapid that further attacks would have hampered friendly forces more than the enemy. The mediums were used against targets in Italy on 21/22 August, after 36 321st Group B-25s had neutralised the battleship *Strasbourg* in Toulon harbour on the 18th. Hit by eight bombs, the *Strasbourg* settled in shallow water, along with a cruiser and a submarine. After a Pantellaria-style bombardment of Ile de Ratonneau and Ile de Pomegues, islands with heavy gun emplacements dominating the seaward approaches to Marseille, the mediums' campaign in southern France was over. On 27 August no less than 58 B-25s and 93 B-26s pounded Ratonneau while 18 B-25s hit Pomegues. Both islands surrendered the following day. By 1 September, those TAC air units still remaining on Corsica had been relocated in Italy.

In the last year of the war the 12th Air Force mediums extended the 'Mallory Major' strikes begun in July against the viaducts and rail bridges of the Italian railway system. For some months these air operations were virtually the only Allied effort as the army picture was still very much static. Primary objectives for the bombers when the Italian offensive was renewed by the 12th was interdiction of the crossing points on the Po River and close support to Allied armies, then poised to assault the Gothic Line.

On 3 September, 112 B-25s cut the rail and road bridges at Casale Monferrato, Chivasso and Torreberetti. A follow-up B-24 attack did more damage on the 5th with the result that all crossings over the Po from Turin in the west to the Adriatic in the east were blocked. To consolidate this

120
Parafrag bombs spew from their carriers as 'lucky' 13 of the 445th BS releases over the Brenner line bridge at Staz die Ceraini, north-west of Verona, 10 March 1945. One of the many century-mission 12th AF Mitchells, 43-27698 did 137 and went home to the US after the war. *USAF*

121
Chewed up: It was probably flak that did this to a 486th Squadron B-25J of the 340th Group, during one of the many missions against the Italian railway system during late 1944-45.

122
This damage definitely wasn't from AA fire, but the result of a mid-air collision. It happened during a January 1945 attack on the Brenner line when another Mitchell in a 340th Group formation sliced into the 488th Squadron machine flown by Lt W. B. Pelton. The squadron made three runs on the target, a railway running alongside a river, and during the turn away the propeller of an aircraft that went down severed the tail guns, ripped along the tailplane and cut the starboard fin and rudder off. Lt Pelton coaxed the stricken B-25 to 13,000ft and headed home to Corsica. After a safe landing, co-pilot H. K. Shackelford said, 'I think God was really the co-pilot'. *John Sutoy*

advantage, the mediums ranged far and wide to isolate the battle area when the US 5th Army opened its offensive on 9 September. Great effort was also made to blast a path through the Gothic Line defences in the face of increasingly bad weather as the last winter of the war began. Rimini presented a difficult obstacle in mid-September and the mediums initiated 'Crumpet II' against the German defences ringing the city. As the 42nd Wing was tied down with operations in the Futa Pass area, it fell to the 57th's Mitchells to execute Crumpet II in concert with the mediums and fighter bombers of the Desert Air Force.

Concentrating its main effort north of the battlefront, mainly along the banks of the Marecchio River, the 57th began with three missions that put a total of 163 tons of frag and demolition bombs down on the enemy before the weather forced a short stand down. The weather closed in completely on the 19th, by which time Allied troops had nearly broken through. Two days later, Rimini was secured and an important breach in the Gothic Line had been opened.

Although it appeared that the end of the war in Italy was in sight, the elements conspired to aid Kesselring far more than he

had a right to expect and the war in that theatre was to drag on for seven months more but at the time, it was felt that the Allies merely had to contain the enemy and mop up as he retreated. Consequently, with the roads and railways under constant surveillance to watch for signs of repair and movement, the air forces waited for the armies to fan out into the Po River valley. For the next few months though, the squadrons would have to await clear conditions before laying on damaging attacks. Under this unexpected ally, the enemy accomplished a good deal to consolidate the ground he still held. Allied plans hinged on deploying the US 5th and British 8th Armies in a pincer movement north and south of Bologna. To break the deadlock, MASAF opened 'Pancake' in far from ideal October weather. Its objective was the destruction of German strongpoints and supplies in the Bologna area. Both the 42nd and 57th Wings were engaged, the B-25s staging a maximum effort on the 12th, a 177-aircraft strike on two supply concentrations, a barracks area and a fuel dump. Hampered by cloud cover, the bombers nevertheless hit most of their objectives. Unfortunately, the ground forces were unable to follow through. Some excellent bombing was achieved in November under Operation 'Harry', but while the mediums bombed both accurately and economically, they could hardly flatten the terrain in front of the troops, tanks and artillery. Neither could they prevent the weather hampering their own efforts or those of their forces on the ground.

There was now some rethinking of strategy in the face of unexpectedly strong German resistance: in order to force the enemy to retreat across the Po and be denied an escape route further north, the four remaining railway lines that ran north of the Po through the Brenner Pass, plus the Tarvisio, Piedicoole and Postumia lines that connected Italy with Austria and Yugoslavia would have to be heavily interdicted. As these lines had to cross four rivers as part of a complex network, it was estimated that this could be done relatively easily.

Medium bombers and heavies went at the job with their now practiced skill and accomplished a temporary closure of the lines. They had to be kept closed and the job eventually fell entirely to the mediums, although there was initially thought of giving the northern routes to the heavy bombers because the terrain and heavy flak defences indicated prohibitive losses among the Mitchell and Marauder squadrons. Conversely, the winter weather

123
Flying over landscape typical
of the 57th Wing's 'beat', these
340th Group B-25Js show the
two forms of camouflage
employed by squadron
aircraft. Nearest the camera is
a factory-finished OD and grey
aircraft, while 43-27657 in the
background has field applied
green upper surfaces over
natural metal finish. The
wing's targets were usually
tiny and often hidden by the
shadows of mountain passes,
mist or cloud and surrounded
by the ever-alert flak. *USAF*

often prevented the heavies from seeing
their cloud covered targets, whereas the
lower altitude mediums were often able to
penetrate the mist and overcast.

Although by late October all the Po River
bridges had been closed, the Germans were
still able to bring supplies down from the
north by ingenious use of pontoons and
ferries, albeit in quantities only large
enough for immediate needs. The trains
were still running north of the Po.

On 3 November a new policy therefore
came into effect. The Po River became sec-
ondary to the Brenner route and the three
north-western river crossings. First
priority was to force the enemy to give up
using the modern, electrified rail system
and revert to slower, steam motive power
for his supply trains — a reduction of about
30 trains per day in each direction to
approximately 10 per day. By bombing the
electricity transformer stations, the 12th
bottled up hundreds of supply wagons and
disrupted the network over large areas,
whereupon, the mediums and fighter

bombers systematically wrecked them and
cut the lines in numerous places. Then the
Bridge Busters went back to the river
crossings, supported by heavy bomber
attacks.

But with the heavies of the 15th Air
Force increasingly needed to deliver the
coup de grace to the industrial centres of
Austria and Germany, the tactical air
forces were given complete charge of communications targets from 16 November. It
selected the targets and carried out the
attacks, its jurisdiction being anywhere in
Italy. There were some 44 medium bomber
missions up to 19 November, the route
through the Brenner Pass remaining closed
until the last days of the month. Most of
December saw a severe curtailment of
operations due to bad weather.

By the end of 1944 there had been some
changes in the composition of the 12th Air
Force medium bomber wings. Pressure to
move the 12th back to France had been
resisted but was partially achieved when
the 42nd Wing's Marauders were trans-

ferred to the ETO and the 319th Group converted from B-26s to B-25s to achieve commonality in the all-Mitchell 57th Wing, a task accomplished very smoothly.

There was no further reduction of medium bomber strength, although more fighter bombers were brought into the interdiction campaign and DAF lent its support, not only to the bombing of rail targets, but stockpiles of supplies. November saw an all out effort against such targets, the Germans losing many thousands of tons of vital stores, especially ammunition, as a result. Other types of target occasionally made a break from the rigours of flying over cloud-covered mountain passes guarded by experienced flak crews. On 23 September for example, the 340th BG was called upon to sink the Italian liner *Taranto* to prevent her being sunk by the Germans in the entrance to La Spezia harbour, where she would have made an effective block ship.

An 18-ship formation put its bombs on target and the liner sank in 25 minutes. General Cannon reported that the attack was the 62nd the group had made without a miss.

Although the Luftwaffe had been conspicious by its absence over northern Italy for months on end, and medium bombers had, since September, been undertaking their missions unescorted, the appearance of the Italian Fascist Republican Air Force in mid-October caused some concern. A few aircraft were lost as a result of interceptions, but the enemy effort was soon contained and stopped altogether. With diversions into Yugoslavia and the static situation on the ground, the 12th's medium bombers were kept busy at the end of 1944 by a sudden German offensive on 26 December. Being only of limited strength it was held and the Allies prepared to settle down for a winter of inactivity before a spring offensive.

Early 1945 was not so quiet for the air forces, which continued interdiction operations in order to prevent the Germans making any gains before the inevitable end. Surrender negotiations were conducted in the spring, the Allies refusing any terms short of unconditional surrender. B-25s and B-26s were still expending hundreds of tons of bombs on the Italian railway system, as were the light bombers of the DAF. Bridges, and open stretches of line were blanketed in a broad sweep of operations that achieved another halt in enemy movement before the final Allied offensive.

Operation 'Wowser' was the final air effort in Italy. It did not, as previously, call for a full air offensive before the ground forces moved but rather a further dose of what had gone before. Indeed by March, so thoroughly had the mediums and fighter bombers interdicted the Italian railway system that they began to seek targets elsewhere, particularly in Yugoslavia and Austria. Also, the run down of the strategic bombing campaign released hundreds of heavy bombers to assist ground operations. The result was that the mediums only attacked Italian targets when specifically requested to do so.

124
Personnel taking five in the shade of a B-25J of the 310th Group. The lack of guns suggest that the photo was taken when the 57th Wing had completed the job.
via R. L. Ward

ThreeViews

The following is a record of answers to a questionnaire circulated to ex-B-25 personnel by the author. All three crewmen served with the 319th Bomb Group in the MTO, A. H. Ahlbrecht with the 440th Squadron and R. E. Casteel and Harold E. Oyster with the 439th. As this group was unique amongst USAAF medium bomber units in operating the B-26 and A-26 as well as the B-25 in combat, each man has been able to make some comparison of the Mitchell with its contemporaries. The written answers have been edited where necessary, but in the main they are verbatim replies.

Q: *Please give brief details of the squadron/group you flew with, your crew position and the number of missions flown.*

Ahlbrecht: 20 missions from 1 November to 1 December 1944. Pilot.

Casteel: 15 B-25 missions. Pilot.

Oyster: August to 31 December 1944 in both B-25 and B-26. Radio Operator-Gunner.

Q: *Can you give impressions of the B-25 as a combat aircraft and compare it with any other combat types?*

Ahlbrecht: I was fortunate enough to fly 25 B-26 and 6 A-26 missions in addition to those with the B-25 — which was much easier to fly than either of the others. I flew my first pilot combat mission with a total time of one hour's training, but I never felt comfortable with a B-26 till I had 300 hours first pilot time. The B-25J was much easier to fly on one engine; the B-26 barely flew on one and the A-26 did nicely. Take

125
Having been wooed away from their beloved B-26s to fly Mitchells as part of the all-B-25 57th Wing, the men of the 319th Group worked hard to lay on the first mission with the new aircraft on 4 November 1944. By the 18th of the month, the group had made it 30 in Mitchells and the 446th mission of the war. The target was the Castel Nova railway bridge and two 440th Squadron aircraft are seen leaving the area.
Harold E. Oyster

off and landing was easy by comparison with the B-26 and formation flying was easier in the Mitchell than either of the others. The B-26 was the hardest to fly but the most rugged, the B-25 the easiest to fly but least rugged. The A-26 was a superb airplane: same bomb load as the others, but 40mph faster; two or three man crew; single engine performance exceptional. The B-25 had no problems with oil coolers (the B-26 was bad in this way) and none with propellers, whereas the B-26s could run away. Wright Cyclone engines were much noisier than Pratt and Whitneys and the B-25 had much less room everywhere than the B-26.

Casteel: I picked up a new B-25J at Tunis on 22 October 1944 after only one previous landing in the type and no take offs. Fortunately, the trip to Corsica didn't require fuel transfer, for I wasn't sure of the procedure! I flew my first B-25 combat mission on Piacenza railroad bridge, Italy, on 16 November 1944.

The B-25 was a good combat aircraft, but not as stable a bombing platform as the B-26. It was slightly faster than the 26 but it had a Chevrolet feel compared to the Cadillac feel of the Martin. Also, the 26 could stand more damage than the 25 — although the Mitchell had better single-engine characteristics. The Douglas A-26 was the best of the three; B-26 next, then the B-25. Later (1952-53) I flew the F-51 and F-80 — and that is where flying really is.

Oyster: The B-25 was a good aircraft and would fly well after sustaining damage to

an engine; this was particularly important over hilly country such as that in Northern Italy. It was noisy, somewhat light and gave a bumpy ride, particularly in rough weather. Movement front to rear over the bomb bay and to the nose through the tunnel was difficult; it was also difficult to get into the bomb bay in case of trouble or other needs. The B-25 was not the best plane for a belly landing because it would split just in front of the turret.

The B-26 Marauder was a more stable aircraft than the B-25 and could take considerable battle damage to all parts except an engine — it would fly on a single engine, but not as well. The B-26 was much better to belly land, due to lengthwise structural ribs and was easier to get in an out of. The B-26 would also sink fast in water, although I'm not certain about the B-25 in this respect. B-25s were more forgiving of sloppy maintenance and/or pilotage but overall I felt that the B-26 was a sturdier aircraft and I felt safer in it over enemy territory.

Q: *While flak and fighters were always dangerous, can you recall a particularly rough mission regarding the attention of either or both?*

Ahlbrecht: The 22 December 1944 mission to a railroad bridge over the Po River was our first mission for several days due to bad weather and additional flak defences had been moved in. The flak was of medium intensity but extremely accurate and we lost two of our four ships, one over the target and one en route home.

Casteel: Roughest mission in the B-25 was

127
Battle Formation: Flying four flights of three aircraft each tucked in close for protection just in case enemy fighters put in an appearance, the 319th goes to war.
via Harold E. Oyster

128
While it had B-26s, the 319th's targets were mainly communications in the Brenner Pass area and up into Yugoslavia. Before the group left for the US and re-assignment to the 7th AF, if flew 76 missions in the B-25. These low-numbered aircraft are from the 437th Bomb Squadron.
via Harold E. Oyster

127

128

on 10 December 1944 over San Michele railroad bridge, Italy — flak and fighters. My tail gunner got an Me 109 and our squadron lost one aircraft and had several severely damaged.

Oyster: We had many rough missions in Northern Italy at that time. The biggest problem was flak, although we were hit by fighters two or three times. My diary shows a mission over Trento — fighters — says 'Pretty hot'. I remember a 20mm went through the tail assembly over the tail gunner's head. We had lots of other hits, too.

One mission, marked Bologna (27 December) — dropping leaflets — says,

'Lots of flak, returned on one engine'. On 10 December we were hit by fighters on the way to San Michele and one plane in our squadron was shot down. We flew a very close formation which helped to give a favourable account of ourselves under fighter attack — this was true for the B-25 as well as other types of aircraft.

Q: *What was generally considered to be the toughest type of target?*

Ahlbrecht: Our group specialised in extremely accurate bombing and we were assigned some very small bridges linking Italy to the supply routes from Germany. The targets like those in the Brenner Pass were well protected by flak and were extremely difficult to hit. We went back to them many times.

Casteel: Railroad bridges important to the enemy — in any area.

Oyster: Two types: (A) Direct ground support for troops when, because of weather, we went in at lower altitudes and thus were more vulnerable to fire from smaller-calibre weapons. (B) Going in in advance of the main bomber force at lower altitudes, to attack anti-aircraft emplacements. They threw everything at you, including the proverbial kitchen sink.

Q: *Did you participate in any missions that departed from the usual pattern?*

Ahlbrecht: I flew a single ship weather mission on 23 December that seemed unique to me after flying in large ship formations. We also flew a long mission from Corsica (our base) across Italy to bomb a key bridge in Yugoslavia. I believe it was a request of the partisans.

Casteel: Not in the B-25.

Oyster: As mentioned in (B) before. Also the missions over Yugoslavia when we carried

129
Nice shot of a 319th Group B-25J in typical markings and configuration. The group tended to leave the lower package gun on each side, whereas other 57th Wing Mitchells dispensed with them altogether. Other armament, including the fixed .50-cal for the pilot, was generally retained. Obvious in this view is the tubular fairing fitted to some J models, presumably for the purpose of cooling or the dispersion of cordite fumes.
via Harold E. Oyster

sidearms in case we were shot down. Another unusual type was when we tried to create landslides in the Brenner Pass areas.

Q: *How did the B-25 stand up to battle damage and was it considered easy to abandon if the need arose?*

Ahlbrecht: I do not believe the B-25 could take flak damage as well as the B-26. My comparison, from my boyhood hunting days, was that a B-26 came down like a mallard duck, fighting all the way, but the B-25 just crumpled and gave up. Conversely, the B-25 flew superbly on one engine compared with the B-26, which barely flew. I believe it was easier to bail out of the B-25 than the Marauder, with the exception that the bombardier had a long tunnel crawl. The A-26, by contrast to both the others, was believed to be almost impossible to abandon.

Casteel: I mentioned that the B-26 could take more hits; the B-25 was easy to abandon.

Oyster: The B-25 would sustain a fair amount of battle damage; of particular importance was its ability to maintain altitude on one engine. It was very tough to get out of the nose: line of sight fore and aft was difficult, so the communication system was important. If it was shot out, those in the rear were not certain what was happening, with the result that they could jump prematurely, or not at all.

Q: *How closely did aircrew liaise with groundcrew over technical matters regarding aircraft performance?*

Ahlbrecht: We would discuss whenever we found a problem and the ground crew would always call a possible problem to our attention before a mission and ask

about it afterwards.

Casteel: Our ground people were the best. They listened. Our in-commission rate was great and they were responsible for our safe return more than we know.

Oyster: We compared notes closely prior to take off and after landing. Otherwise we were in different areas due to time of working hours.

Q: *How was mission planning generally regarded by crews and was intelligence on targets, defences and weather conditions adequate?*

Ahlbrecht; Planning was excellent and defences were almost always known exactly.

Casteel: Exellent.

Oyster: For the times, I would say good. Naturally everybody complained — but this type of warfare was relatively new and crews were really not professional types. Most of them had a minimum amount of time in any aircraft, let alone a complex bomber formation. We used a single aircraft on weather reconnaissance several hours ahead of the mission to obtain valid conditions over the mainland.

Q: *What was your most lasting impression of operational flying?*

Ahlbrecht: Formation flying was intensely hard work and boring. It was always better, however, to be bored with a milk run than the hot target. 'Bombs away' and the high speed turning dive out of the target areas was what we waited for as we sat there on the 20 second bombing run. When the flak bursts were red and very black, they were too, too close.

13

Casteel: Exciting — thrilling — a challenge — a duty.

Oyster: Close formations for mutual protection. The closeness, need of trust and reliance on other members of the crew and the group, and confidence in your pilot. This all developed a camaraderie and esprit de corps that has been lasting.

Q: *What were living conditions like in your theatre(s) of war?*

Ahlbrecht: Adequate on Corsica. We lived in tents that most of us were able to floor. We kept warm with gas stoves, got a shower once or twice a month, went to Bastia once a month and rest camp every three months. Food was not very good and beer, candy, and cigarettes were rationed but adequate.

Casteel: Adequate — good food — some cognac — remember it was late 1944.

Oyster: From tents made of blankets in Africa to rude houses constructed by natives on Sardinia (we were there for almost a year) — tents on Corsica — tents on Okinawa. It seemed to be either very dry and sandy, or very muddy — snow on Corsica; mosquitoes; rats — but better than front line trenches.

Q: *How did you feel that your squadron compared with others in the group?*

Ahlbrecht: Our squadron and all the others performed at a very high level. We put the planes up as requested and hit our targets without fail. I feel the 319th was an exceptional group and performed very well over a long period of time with three different aircraft.

Casteel: We were tops — great espirit de corps.

Oyster: Everybody thought his squadron was the best one. Inter-squadron competitiveness helped develop this spirit, although we all knew that we were an integral part of the whole.

In addition to the foregoing, Harold Oyster offered this note about interservice co-operation:

'In April 1944, we had an exchange programme whereby infantry officers would visit our base to see our operations and also to fly with us, while some of our men went to the front lines, to develop an appreciation of each other's role. Also, in the case of close ground support of infantry, they would fly with us and our people would be in the front lines, for identification purposes. It was a thrill to think you helped the boys in the trenches. A case in point was Faenza, 21-24 November inclusive, when we flew ten missions bombing defence areas just ahead of the troops. One day there was complete cloud cover — no drop. Next day we went in much lower and dropped bombs, but sustained much flak damage. Later communications said we did a lot of damage to enemy troops and enabled Allied forces to cross a river.'

130
Waist gunner's view of a 440th Squadron formation over rugged Italian terrain. The difficulty in locating targets can well be appreciated.
via Harold E. Oyster

Have Guns,Will Travel   Bill Goodrich

W. S. 'Bill' Goodrich was a pilot with the 17th Reconnaissance Squadron from October 1944 until the end of the war. Despite its designation, the 17th operated mainly as a close support bombing and strafing outfit and was to quote Bill, 'a bastard squadron which worked under 5th Fighter Command'. Only once, he recalls, did the unit's B-25s fly a mission with a bomber group, when it joined the 38th for a strike to Hainan Island on 14 March 1945. For Bill Goodrich it was a highly memorable trip.

'The briefing we had just finished left all of us with that rock-in-the-stomach feeling when you know the target is going to be another very tough one. Our assigned target for tomorrow was the Samah airdrome on Hainan Island off the China coast, which had been a major Japanese staging airfield for attacks all over the South China Sea.

'It had been in Japanese hands for a number of years, so we knew it to be most heavily defended. We were attached to the 38th (low level) Bomb Group which was up on Luzon to add more strafers against the target. The fact that we had photographs of the strip taken the day before from a P-38 was not a hell of a lot of comfort, as they showed dozens of fighters sitting in revetments and parked on the ramp, plus numerous extremely heavy ack ack positions. We were then equipped with the J-32 model strafer with 12 forward-firing .50 calibre guns which were depressed 6 degrees and vortexed 600ft ahead, each gun firing 750 rounds a minute. With that kind of firepower we could knock down a building, sink a ship or just create merry hell on the ground ahead of us. We alway considered that two B-25J-32s flying wingtip to wingtip and strafing and skip bombing were an even bet against a destroyer.

'However, to do this job right, a group of B-24s from somewhere — we never did know exactly — was scheduled to procede out attack time by five minutes and bomb the target from high altitude, a tactic that breaks up a field pretty well. We would then scoot through at ground level, shoot up everything and skip bomb with napalm, which normally was a very efficient method of messing up an airfield.

'When planning our strike, the target run was figured for the best attacking direction, using any hills, trees and buildings as cover so that our approach was a surprise until we broke out into the open. Any run was made as low as we could get, preferably getting our propeller tips green from cutting grass (which isn't as much of a lie as it sounds) because the defender had a big problem hitting a target moving at about 300mph at very low level. His gun was usually blocked by some kind of obstruction as you went by him. Most ground defence was done by having gunners go under cover, aim the barrels straight up and hold the trigger open. The effect was like trying to fly through a fire hose without getting wet. As the saying goes, ''There ain't no way''. We got holes but mostly in non-vital places. Very exciting, but not condusive to a healthy old age.

'We took off in our 12 B-25s from the dirt strip on Mindoro Island about 3pm to fly up to Lingayen strip, a steel mat laid on the beach on Luzon, the home of the 38th Bomb Group. After checking in and drawing a cot and a blanket, which I set up as my sleeping quarters for the night, I went looking for a poker game. As normal, I found an open spot at a high stakes table and had a good run, picked up several hundred dollars plus a lot of jungle juice and at about 2am, decided to go sack out. Got back to where I had set up my cot only to find some bastard had swiped it. After much scrounging around in the dark, I found a cot with no end bars. Not good, but at least I was off the ground which had an amazing array of crawling creatures. We were awakened at 5am to a breakfast of field kitchen pancakes which, due to the number of crew members to be fed and the few field stores available, were burned to a charred black outside and when cut, the insides ran out raw.

'Now being completely bright eyed, bushy-tailed, rested and well fed as all pilots are when leaving on a combat mission (any service manual will tell you this), we climbed into our planes ready as we would ever be.

'Our take off was uneventful and we formed a very loose formation, climbed to 6,000ft for the four-hour flight to the target. This was to be a very long flight for B-25s, estimated at almost $8\frac{1}{2}$ hours, which was the absolute extreme. When we were about 50 miles from Hainan, we dropped down to about 50ft to be below radar pick up.

'When we finally sighted Hainan, it was obvious that the heavies had not been there. No smoke, nothing. Also, to make matters worse, a Jap task force of cruisers and destroyers had moved in since the recon photos and were berthed right alongside the airfield. If there was ever anything we didn't need, it was all that additional firepower against us.

'The group leader then did the most foolish thing that could have been done. He decided to circle the flight and wait for the big bombers. As we began to swing into a wide left turn, fighter planes started to climb out and up. Our surprise was blown higher than hell. We came around to our original heading and our leader came on the radio saying we would go in and make our run as planned. This was to come in low on the eastern tip of the island, drop into trail at 10-second intervals, come through a large canyon which opened on to a flat plain about five miles wide on which the airfield was built. We would strafe and bomb the length of the field, including hangars, planes and buildings, tailoring our individual flightpath to what the planes ahead has not hit.

'That big swing round, alerting the fighters, almost did us in. Our approach through the canyon was as obvious to the Japs as it had been to us and, with the element of surprise gone, every gun on the field plus all the big guns of the task force were aimed right on to the mouth of the valley. This, with fighters circling above like vultures waiting for the kill, is what we ran into.

'Because the 17th was attached to the 38th, we were the trailing ships at the end of the line. As I came out of the canyon into flak and very heavy concentrations of all kinds of bursting shells, I could see that the front-runners had done a good job. Buildings were burning, planes on the ground — some were ours — burning and the damned task force, which was to our left, was shooting the hell out of us.

131
Bill Goodrich (left) with 'Andy' Anderson, crew chief of *Mitch the Witch* right through her impressive combat career with the 17th Recon Squadron. Bill flew the veteran B-25D (42-97293) only on what he describes as a few easy missions, because it lacked the heavy firepower of strafer Mitchells, and had hand-charged guns that were prone to jamming — a couple usually went out just as the aircraft was on a target run!
Bill Goodrich

131

'I was about halfway through the run when there was a tremendous explosion and my plane went into a hard right steep climbing turn. My airspeed was about 325mph as I was maybe 20-30ft high, I tried to correct by opposite rudder and full forward correction but almost nothing happened. I could hear pinging sounds which meant more holes in us and another big bang as the corrections started to nose the plane over at about 500ft. As she came over the top and straightened out some, I was able to catch her on the balance point by going to full opposite rudder and elevator, then catching her again until the diving and yawing was corrected by degrees.

'We had no more than come under partial control, and I was edging toward the ocean, when a flight of four Zero fighters which I had noticed about 6,000ft and 1 o'clock, peeled over and started a frontal diving run at us. I'm sure that they figured us a dead cripple as they came down towards us, I held the .50 calibre nose gun trigger open, which poured a path of tracers and bullets ahead of us. One of the Zeros started to smoke and broke away. I think he crashed as we were only 400ft high by then, leaving no room for a downward breakaway. The others broke off and climbed around for a tail attack. For 15 minutes they tried to knock us off balance; they had put a lot more holes in us when I saw a flight of five B-25s just above our level going away. We were still going flat out and I flew right under that flight. The fighters decided not to try any more and went home, leaving us with a long flight to go.

'Our radios were not working but the intercom was and I called back to the gunner to ask if he could see any damage, as the plane was extremely sloppy on her controls. He said, "Jesus Christ, Lieutenant, the whole right tail section and rudder is gone. The waist gun was blown right out through the side of the ship and we're full of holes. Are we going to ditch?"

'I told him, "Hell no, I can't swim that far."

'Besides, I didn't quite believe his statement about the stabiliser and rudder although I knew something was seriously wrong.

'The flight we had joined kept with us and very carefully and slowly climbed up to 5,000ft for the flight home. I did some very gentle turns and up and down manoeuvres just to see what control I did have. Not much. Any change from straight and level and it was against the stops corrections until oscillating stopped. I figured that as long as she was in balance

we would fly home OK, but if we ran into a weather front it would by "Katy bar the door" because no way could we correct for rough air. Luckily, we had good weather all the way.

'I planned that when we got back, we would bail-out close to the beach and let the plane go. But, after a couple hours of thinking about it, and not being too inclined to trust a parachute, I thought maybe I'd try to land her.

'I talked this over with my crew on the intercom and suggested that as we made our approach they were to take crash positions, which means sit on the floor backed against the back wall of the bomb bay, and the moment they felt the wheels touch, everybody run as far back in the tail as possible to keep the load off the front wheel until we slowed a bit. Then I was reasonably sure that we could land, park it, and walk away.

'As we neared home base at Lingayen, several planes came up to look us over as the flight which was baby-sitting us had radioed ahead. We were expected and as the strip appeared we could see we had quite an audience waiting to see what would happen. I figured that we might as well give them a close look and after firing a couple of red flares for an ambulance pick up, flew a couple of miles down the beach, slowly turned, eased down to a couple of hundred feet and buzzed the strip. I bought a dressing down from the base commander for that, but what the hell, it didn't seem right not to prove it would fly.

'So far, so good; now all we had to do was land. It was a certainty I could not slow down or use flaps because I couldn't keep the nose up, so I flew about five miles down the beach again, eased around and still holding 200ft and 180mph, lined up on the runway, crossed my fingers and dropped the wheels, wondering what she would do. It worked out fine except I had to pull full stick back in my lap just to counteract the wheel drag and add more throttle to keep the nose up so I would be able to fly her straight on to the ground. No go around — had to be right first time. By juggling the throttles the ground level approach looked OK and just before we touched, I hit full throttle which got the nose up enough for the main gear to hit first, snapped off power, shut idle cut-off to windmill the props to help slow down, and slid to a stop with no runway left. I taxied back to the mat strip, got out and looked — and damn near crapped. My gunner was right. No stabiliser and no rudder on the right side. If I had known it for real, I'd probably have crashed because any fool knew a B-25 would just not fly in that condition.

'As it turned out, the two men in the rear compartment had had quite a time over the target. The tail gunner was firing from his position when the tail section got shot off about 12 inches from his seat. He had two pieces of flak in his arm but was flying again two days later. My radioman gunner was firing out of the right side port when what was probably a 40mm shell burst inside the ship. It blew the .50 cal machine gun out of his hands and right through the side of the ship along with his pistol and holster off his hip. The shell also tore the radio section apart but didn't scratch him.

'We got the next day off for rest and relaxation, were issued a new plane and away we went for another 50 missions. I flew 78 in all, 76 of them credited as combat missions, between 18 October 1944 (my first) and the last on 20 August 1945. That was a four-plane shipping sweep from Ie Shima to southern Japan, the aircraft being armed to strike anything we saw. The war was called off by radio during the mission, so we salvoed our bombs into the ocean, turned around and buzzed back to base, happy as hell.

'From the records, I note that 30 of my missions were ground support using from one to six planes, a job that requried strafing and napalm attack ahead of advancing or pinned-down infantry. Getting target info was simple; we flew from metal mat strips in forward positions and lived with the infantry in tents and slit trenches. They kept a perimeter guard around the area which usually followed MacArthur's dictum of only taking the ground you need. On most islands, we controlled a small area and it was the responsibility of air to keep enemy resupply out. As we lived with the ground forces, they only had to tell us what had to be hit, show us on their contour maps and generally mark the area with smoke shells for us to clobber the target.

'Reconnaissance missions show in the log as 29. Again one to six planes were used and as all missions were armed for targets of opportunity, they were generally fun. Trains, cars, small ships, warehouses etc, were hit. We also flew a couple of night weather recon flights.

'There were 14 missions to Formosa. These were the tough ones, mainly against shipping, airfields or other targets assigned. The island was heavily fortified and we always got holes in our planes and lost quite a few. Up to 12 aircraft flew these surprise attacks, some of them at night. There were two missions to knock out highway and rail bridges by skip

bombing with 1,000 pounders. The second one was successful.

'We were in an island-hopping war, never long on any one and most of our recon was to new areas. We left New Guinea in mid-October 1944 and went to Tacloban and Dulang on Leyte; to Minoro; Luzon and finally, Ie Shima by July 1945. We spent about three months on Iwo, less in other locations.

'I think our toughest mission was while we were based on Mindoro. All our forces were taking such a beating that it looked like we might get pushed out of the Philippines a second time. The 17th and two fighter squadrons, one with P-40s, the other with P-47s, was sent to Mindoro, which is just below Manilla harbour, to stop the flow of Jap supplies by sea. And we sunk enough of them for a battle fleet to be sent down to take us out. A heavy cruiser, six destroyers, a submarine and many support ships were spotted by a Navy plane at 3pm. There was no question as to where the force was headed.

'Our CO wisely decided that we had no chance in daylight so we just sat and waited for them — a perfect example of "sweating it out". At that time we were flying from a dusty dirt strip on the beach which came within big gun range of the fleet shortly after dark. Before and during the naval bombardment, which went on for 30 minutes, we attacked the fleet, going in low on the water. We skip bombed without using guns while fighters diving in shooting to draw the ships' fire upwards. The targets were so close to the strip that we never even got our wheels up. It was the damndest fight you could ever imagine.

'After about an hour we had no more bombs, no ammo and very little gas. We filled up with what was left and took off for Leyte. Weather was bad getting there and of 18 planes that started, only five made it to Leyte. Five were lost in battle and the rest got lost or ran out of gas and ditched. As I remember, six crews were returned to us by local sympathisers some days later.

'Those who made it were rearmed and sent back to Mindoro to pick up the attack. As we were only five planes, I always figured that the general in charge was going to have the 17th Squadron wiped out to simplify the paperwork.

'Anyway, when we came in low behind Mindoro for a surprise run across the hills, not a ship was to be seen in the whole ocean. We circled around and landed between craters and wrecks to be met by our ground people whom we had had to leave the night before. Afterwards they told us that just as we had left for Leyte, the Japanese fleet also turned and ran.

Both sides had taken casualties and we came up with a draw. But we still held the island.*

'The best shipping strike I ever flew on was about my third or fourth mission against a Jap re-supply convoy coming at us on Leyte. I don't remember who was flight leader, but in my opinion the attack was perfect.

'We had 12 planes. I was flying wing on the leader and had been told to stay wing-to-wing with him. The convoy was found sailing parallel to a coastal mountain range. Our flight leader took us up a valley behind the mountains, popping up at intervals to keep the ships in sight. When we were about opposite to them we came over the mountains to achieve complete surprise. We dived almost to sea level to pick up 300mph air speed.

'There were four troop ships and several supply vessels in the convoy, guarded by destroyers and gun ships and, even with surprise on our side, we took a lot of flak. We got holed, lost one plane and I learned a great deal. We were skip bombing with 500 pounders using four to five second delay fusing. I had been told to fly with the

*The action described above was the last sortie by the IJN into the Philippines area. The task force consisted of the heavy cruiser *Ashigara*; the light cruiser *Oyoda* and destroyers *Kiyoshimo*, *Asashimo*, *Kaya*, *Sugi*, *Kashi* and *Kasumi*. The *Oyoda* was slightly damaged by two direct hits and the *Kiyoshimo* was later sunk by PT boats after bombs had hit her twice and caused heavy damage. The action achieved nothing.

leader even though I was new to this game — and I soon found out why.

'As the leader dove to make his target run on the first supply ship, I slipped behind him quite a bit. He made a perfect hit — on an ammunition ship. It went up in an explosion that probably reached 4,000ft, right in front of me. I can still remember that huge ball of flame in which I could see "I" beams spinning as I flew into it. Went right through and didn't hit anything, but I never, never got behind the leader again. It was one of the things that convince you that the older combat flyers have reasons for what they tell you to do.

'When I joined the 17th, I recall that we had glass nosed B-25s with field installed .50s. I flew the B, C, D, G, H and J models during the war and my opinion of the B-25 was simply, great. It was rugged and fast with tremendous firepower. We all liked the planes for strafing. All our missions were armed reconnaissance with the pilot choosing to attack or not and it was not until early 1945 that we used hand-held cameras (Fairchild F.27s I think) to take pictures.

'Early in 1945, the 17th was offered the A-26 Invader. We three flight leaders flew one mission in it, but decided to stay with the B-25. Although the A-26 was 40mph faster, the engines were mounted forward of the pilot, giving about 100 degree visibility forward. But our wing-to-wing pattern in the B-25s gave us about 180 degrees plus — which for us was more important than the greater speed of the A-26.'

132
Mitch leads a younger 17th Squadron B-25J over a target, dropping parafrags. No less than 172 missions are marked in the previous photograph, although Bill Goodrich believes she flew more than 190 — they weren't shown because credits were not painted on during the latter stages of the war. Everyone was delighted that *Mitch* saw the end of the war and Bill believes that she ended up on a Pacific island scrapheap.

Pacific War

133
Blast and B-25 slipstream
ripple the palm trees bordering
the runway of Alexishaven
airfield as the 5th Air Force
chalks up another enemy
aircraft destroyed. *USAF*

134
A 71st Squadron Mitchell
takes to the hills after a strike
on Tuligan Harbour in western
New Guinea. *via Bruce Hoy*

135
Alexishaven suffers again as
the Tigers carry out a blanket
parafrag attack. Over 80
bombs drift down as an 823rd
Bomb Squadron B-25G
completes its run.
via Bruce Hoy

136
Dagua, New Guinea burning under a shower of deadly mushrooms from 501st Bomb Squadron B-25s. Unwisely, the Japanese chose to line their aircraft up in the centre of the field rather than disperse them and the Mitchell on the extreme left has aimed for the four Ki-61s in the centre of the photograph. A further 'Tony', two 'Oscars' and two 'Helen' bombers can just be discerned through the smoke.
Robert H. Strauss

137
Supporting the ground forces' operations to secure Capt Gloucester on New Britain, the 501st Squadron worked over Japanese positions along the shoreline . . .

138
. . . and the airfield. Bomb bay doors agape and strike cameras ready to roll, six strafers make their run over the lunar-like surface, well plastered in previous air attacks.
Both USAF via Frank F. Smith

93

139

Attacking off Wewak, a 71st Squadron strafer pours on the coal after skip bombing a merchantman. *USAF*

141

140

Happy Hunting Ground: 5th AF strafers found plenty of targets in Hansa Bay, northwest of Alexishaven, including camouflaged schooners. With the sea subsiding after sending up geysers from previous bomb runs, a 22nd Bomb Group B-25D (41-30434) comes in for another pass, just to make sure. *USAF*

142

141

Bloody Bismarck: When the Japanese sent a large reinforcement convoy to Lae in March 1943, the 5th Air Force sent almost every available aircraft out to stop it. Spearheading the attack were the B-25 strafers of the 3rd Attack's 90th Bomb Squadron, which, supported ably by the RAAF and other USAAF units, wrecked the last (as it turned out) enemy attempt to re-supply his forces in New Guinea. In this photograph, B-25s pounce on freighter in the Bismarck Sea, scene of the carnage that resulted in less than 1,000 (out of 7,000) troops reaching their objective. *USAF*

142

No Hiding Place: Lt Carl Cessna's *Stingeroo* attacking a convoy escort during the series of raids in February 1944 to reduce Kavieng, New Ireland. Both the 38th and 345th took part and on the 16th, the Air Apaches found a 14-ship convoy off New Hanover. While other aircraft completely destroyed the tanker *Taisyo Maru*, Cessna made a skip bombing and strafing run. Dead in the water, the vessel settled by the stern and was photographed in that condition when the Mitchells returned to the area next day. *USAF*

Two Group

H. G. Fitzpatrick

'I joined No 226 Squadron at Swanton Morley, Norfolk in June 1942 as a nav/. bomb aimer in one of the replacement crews needed after the Dieppe operation. Apart from six months "operational rest" as an instructor at No 1482 B&G Flight (later No 2 GpSU) and six weeks in October to December 1942 when I, in common with 24 other navigators from 2 Group squadrons, was seconded to the USAAF for the North African landings, I stayed with No 226 until its disbandment in October/November 1945.

'The first time I saw a Mitchell I was more than disappointed. Here we were flying Bostons, which both looked and flew like birds and we had to give them up — not for Mosquitos — but for what? Standing in the rain with its characteristic hump-backed look, with water dripping off the camera cowling in the tail and from the covered .30-calibre gun hanging down through the front of the bomb-aimer's position in the nose, the wings with dihedral, anhedral, dihedral all dripping with water, made it look as dejected as we were and well deserving of the name on the side, *Dumbo*. It took a long time for this feeling of dejection and disappointment to go away but at the end, we got to like it a lot and some very good work was done by Mitchell squadrons. Perhaps the best thing in its favour was that it could take a lot of stick and still come back. This is perhaps best illustrated by the fact that when I first joined the squadron, operating on Bostons in the low-level or cloud-cover roles, the length of the tour of operations was 25 sorties and you were very lucky to complete a full tour, whereas by March 1945, the operational tour for Mitchell crews had been increased to 85 sorties. There are quite a lot of old 2 Group aircrew who owe their survival to having been re-equipped with Mitchells!

'I think it is true to say that it was only crews who came off Bostons who felt this sense of disappointment. No 305, who came off Wellingtons, thought they were wonderful right from the start, as did No 320, who came off Catalinas. Crews who came over from the Ventura thought they had come to a new world, as indeed they had — or rather they had a much longer stay in this world than they would have had if they had retained Venturas.

'The main disadvantages the Mitchell had in comparison to the Boston were a slower cruising speed, a much slower rate of climb, slower reaction to the throttle and the requirement to adjust fore and aft trim when crew members moved in front of or behind the C of G. The undercarriage handle was so far back that when a pilot reached for it after take-off there was a tendency for him to put the aircraft into a climbing turn to starboard — not very comfortable in a formation take-off. There was also a great problem when flying in the No 3 position, as the pilot could not see his leader because of the wide expanse of the co-pilot's right hand seat. To be fair, these were not so much faults of the aircraft, as it was designed to be (and in the USAAF was) flown with a crew of seven, whereas we only operated with a crew of four except on certain missions when we would carry an extra signaller, gunner or Gee-H operator. We overcame this disadvantage by having the navigator sit in the co-pilot's seat for take-off and landing, and operating flaps and undercarriage controls under the direction of his pilot and putting the more experienced crews in the No 3 position so that they would formate, not on the leader, but on the No 2 man, who could be seen quite easily. I did hear that some USAAF and Dutch crews flew the No 3 position from the right hand seat, but I never saw it with our own crews.

'The early Mitchells were equipped with the sighting head only of the Mk XIV bombsight, whereas the Bostons had the old Mk IX Course Setting Sight, which we only used for "Circuses" and "Ramrods". For low-level missions, every nav/b had his own device. (My own was a chinagraph line drawn across the clear vision nose panel between the second rivets up from the bottom. With my shoulders pressed back against the rear bulkhead and with my pilot holding 240mph — we did not use knots until later — and a height of 20 to 25ft above the ground, I could guarantee to put eight out of ten bombs inside the target triangle. For live targets, I used this system or else pressed the button when my pilot had to lift to go over the target without ballooning. Using this latter method, which allowed for the skip, we could put four bombs up the wall of a power station or a hangar from the ground up to the roof.) When equipped only with the Mk XIV sighting head, we were very restricted. The bombing angle had to be calculated before we took off and this meant that the

143
Tight as a Drum: Mitchell IIs of No 226 Squadron RAF flying the kind of close formation that 2 Group crews were renowned for. Nearest the camera is *Stalingrad*, FV905. *IWM*

bombing height, speed and heading was therefore pre-empted. In turn this meant of course, that there could be no evasive action within some three minutes or so from the aiming point and if there was a difference in the forecast wind speed and direction, there was little real chance of hitting the target. Since we operated at the best level for the 88 and 105mm flak, we were rather like sitting ducks. Later, when we were given the computer box for the Mk XIV sight, the Mitchell proved to be one of the most stable bombing platforms that could be provided.

'It was soon obvious that with the Mitchell the traditional 2 Group tactics would need to be changed. Acceleration was very sluggish compared to both the Boston and the Blenheim, but at the same time, there was little reaction to the throttle, so that once speed was built up, it was very difficult to lose it, making flying in close formation very difficult. When the lower turret was extended it reduced the speed by about 15mph and when the bomb doors were opened, the back of the bomb bay, which was about 50sq ft, acted as a very effective airbrake. However, it was the low rate of climb that really caused us to change our tactics.

'The first time we operated on Mitchells we were on a "Circus" and used our standard lo-hi-lo approach to get in under the German radar cover. Twelve minutes from the target, we started to climb in order to attack from 10,000ft. With everything racing, we crossed over the target at just under 4,000ft — and took the biggest pasting we had experienced for a long time. We had to abandon these tactics and

from then on made certain that we had gained bombing altitude well before we reached the target area. This of course, meant that our fighter escort was faced with a new problem; and we had rapidly to learn the art of co-ordinating evasive action from flak and fighters whilst at the same time allow for a good steady bomb run and a steady platform from which to pour out a heavy curtain of .50in machine gun fire at any attacking fighters which got through our close escort.

'When Basil Embry assumed command of 2 Group about June 1943, we became a force to be reckoned with — better organised, better planned and much better led. We still took targets that no-one else would touch, but it was now a case of being given targets that no-one else could take. We began to operate, not as a small and insignificant force of six aircraft, but as a squadron or wing of three squadrons and sometimes as a two-wing force of 72 or even 96 aircraft on the same target or target area.

'Operating at that strength, we did not need a close escort and normally only had a fighter sweep in the vicinity of the target as were bombing and to cover us on the breakaway. "Circuses" were things of the past and every target we went for was of prime importance and had to be attacked, irrespective of opposition or losses. There was one proviso — no target in occupied France, Belgium or Holland could be attacked if the cloud cover was more than six-tenths or could not be visually sighted and identified up to the point of bomb release. For any crew who broke these regulations — and there was always

144
A standard Mitchell II, FL185
survived the war, being struck
off charge in 1947 after
service with No 180
Squadron.
Aeroplane Monthly

photographic evidence — it meant two weeks in Brighton or Sheffield Aircrew Disciplinary Centres and starting your tour of operations again from scratch.

'From about July/August 1943, the Mitchell wings were almost entirely concentrated on "Ski" targets. They were very difficult to find and required literally pinpoint accuracy. The launching ramp for the flying bombs was very small and narrow and the non-magnetic shed through which all the V-1s had to pass for course setting, was less than half the size of a Nissen hut. I remember one target in the forest of Crecy being given to me as being "200 metres past the bridge, turn left along a footpath. About 500 metres along this path there is a bridle path crossing it at right angles. The entrance to the site is about one kilometer to the left along the bridle path!" Imagine trying to find that from 10,000ft in summer with the trees in full green and half-covered by strato-cu! Often we only located the targets because of the flak they pushed up at us.

'By this time, we had been equipped with the B-25J, which had no bottom turret and the upper turret moved forward of the bomb bay. This modification was a great improvement and increased manouevrability, cruising speed and stability. At about the same time, we were equipped with the full computer box for the Mk XIV bombsight, Gee and blind approach equipment. From then on we operated at medium level (10 to 15,000ft) and had to put in night flying and a lot of instrument flying. Later we were equipped to use Gee-H (for which we carried extra, specialist operators) and from October 1944 often operated under ground control for bombing within 1,000 yards of our own troops. As the Boston squadrons did not have the room to fit the Mk XIV sight and computer box or Gee-H in their aircraft, it became the practice for a Mitchell crew from No 226 to lead in five Bostons from the other two squadrons in the wing, Nos 88 and 342. This gave us great delight as No 88 had always been our rival and No 342 had taken our Bostons.

'When I had first joined the squadron back in 1942, it was the custom for each navigator (or observers as we then were) to take his own sight and release point within the confines of the leader's run. By the middle of 1943 this practice had stopped and the lead crew was responsible for navigation, the control of evasive action and the bombing. Other crews in the formation merely carried out the orders of the leader, given over the R/T by the navigator, gunnery controller or pilot as appropriate. This improved both the accuracy and the bomb pattern but made it very difficult to train leaders. Often a first-class pilot had a navigator who was useless at bombing, or a gunner who had no idea of how to control a formation, even though his own gunnery results were excellent. Sometimes it was the pilot who, although being a brilliant flier, had no idea of how to lead a close formation in the face of intense flak and was a liability to the rest of the aircraft he was leading. Sometimes such men learned quickly and the hard way. One squadron leader who came to use from Bomber Command with a brilliant record, lost three crews in his own formation through absolute clottishness on the part of himself or his observer — we never did find out which as they both blamed each other. However, after a spell with No 1482 Flight and a change of observer, the pilot became a first class squadron and wing leader and did not lose another crew for the rest of the war.

'From March 1944, by which time the squadrons had moved into their wing bases in southern England, until the invasion of France, the Mitchell squadrons operated against road and rail centres, power stations, airfields and coastal defences in a series of concerted raids with Mosquitos and fighter bombers of the 2nd Tactical Air Force, often in conjunction with the US 8th and 9th Air Forces. This really was the beginning of 'round the clock' bombing, with the RAF heavies covering the night phase. As the daylight hours increased, the squadrons were called upon for bigger and better efforts and often as many as three missions a day were mounted by Mitchell squadrons.

'Not all these missions counted towards the crews' operational tours, as they did not count unless the bombs were dropped on target and the restrictions outlined earlier still held. During this period the skies over France were very crowded and navigators had need of new skills to lead a two-wing formation (12 to 18 boxes of six aircraft each) into the target, give each box leader a chance to select his own aiming point, avoid the main flak concentrations and not to be forced out of position by Mos-

quitos and fighters flying below him, the 9th AF at about the same level and the 8th AF above. With over a thousand aircraft operating in the same target area, the sky can be very crowded! I missed most of this phase when I became an instructor, to rejoin No 226 as a member of a lead crew in September 1944.

'During the invasion the Mitchell squadrons reverted to their traditional role of close direction and indirect support to ground forces by attacking strong points, road and rail centres, troop concentrations and so forth. Some crews even laid smoke to protect HMS *Warspite* and other capital ships bombarding coastal defences. From what I heard, the navy had not improved their aircraft recognition and the smoke layers were more likely to be shot down by the ships they were attempting to screen than by enemy guns.

'During the period of closing the Falaise gap after the breakout beyond Caen, Mitchells were given an additional role, that of illuminator for night interdictor Mosquitos. Bombed up with bundles of reconnaissance flares, 56 to a bundle and each flare with an intensity of several thousand candle power, the idea was that the Mitchell would fly to the target area at about 8-10,000ft while a pair of Mosquitos would come in at low level. When all aircraft were in position the Mosquito pilots would call for a light. The Mitchell crew would then carry out a bombing run and drop the flares, by the light of which the

145
Nice view of a No 98 Squadron Mk II edging close into the camera aircraft. As can be seen, the aircraft retains the Bendix lower turret in common with the majority of RAF Mitchells — it seems there were more concert virtuosos in the British service than Jimmy Doolittle reckoned there were in AAF! *IWM*

145

Mossies would attack with cannon and bombs and rockets according to their loads. Each Mitchell would make six or eight runs, not necessarily on the same aiming point. Both types of aircraft were replaced as their ammuntion and flares were exhausted, making it possible to maintain attacks on enemy soft-skinned vehicles, tanks and troops throughout the night.

'This form of co-operation was Mosquitos led to one hilarious sortie. A Mitchell crew had got into position at the rendezvous and was waiting for their pair of Mossies. It should be noted that by now, many of the Mitchells were the Mk III (B-25J) version with a tail gun position where the old photographic fairing had been. I should also mention that there was a large number of Me210s operating in the area, against the marauding Mosquitos. On this particular night, weather was clamping down at the base airfield and only one Mosquito called in at rendezvous. He requested a light and after the Mitchell crew had released one bundle of flares, said that he still could not see. A second flare run was made with the same response from the Mosquito. The Mitchell skipper decided to drop two bundles on the next run, with the result that it was brighter than daylight, and even the Mitchell crew could see targets. It was obvious that the Mosquito was out of position so the Mitchell circled, waiting for him to arrive. Eventually the Mosquito appeared and another flare run was made — again with two bundles. Still the Mossie crew remained blind. By this time it was rather unhealthy around the Mitchell as the German flak crews were having themselves a ball — it was not every night that they had a target which illuminated itself with light brighter than any of their searchlights or which stayed in the flak zone for so long. Two more runs (112 flares) were to no avail. Finally the Mitchell skipper blew his top and as soon as he had released the last last two bundles, he stuck the nose down, partly to get out of the flak and partly to attack with gunfire from his turret to show this "ruddy Mossie crew where the ruddy targets were!" It was a wonderful idea but the results were sheer comic opera.

'The turret gunner of the Mitchell then called out "Bandits" and reported an Me210 closing fast. From there right back to the UK there was a running fight between the Mitchell and "Me210". At one stage the skipper of the Mitchell called up the pilot of the Mosquito and said, "You've done nothing else all night so for God's sake come and take this thing off my tail."

146

'The Mosquito pilot replied, "I'll come as soon as I can but I've got me a Dornier 215 I'm dealing with." The fight was inconclusive and the Mitchell landed at Hartford Bridge and the Mosquito at Lasham, both having received hits, but not too much damage. Later when the aircraft were examined, it was proved that hits on both had been caused by Allied calibre fire, not German. It was obvious that the "210" was in fact the Mosquito and that the Mitchell, with its forward turret had been mistaken by the Mosquito pilot as a Do215. We reckoned that this was the only occasion when the attacker and target were in continuous R/T contact during an engagement.

'The Mitchell could take a lot of punishment from flak and fighters, although after one or two attacks at the time we were operating on single box missions, the German fighters left us severely alone, for it took a lot of courage for a fighter to attack a multi-unit formation at squadron, wing or two-wing strength. We flew much closer than USAAF formations and there was no room for a fighter to get between

146
Commanders: During the planning for 'Overlord', there was much discussion between the Allied air commanders on how best to employ airpower before, during and after the great invasion. In April 1944 Air Marshall Sir Arthur Coningham, AOC 2nd Tactical Air Force (left) and Gen Lewis Brereton, Commander of the 9th AAF, did the rounds of 2 Group's Mitchell bases. *IWM*

147
Fully kitted up, W/O C. V. Fenwick poses under the dorsal turret guns of a 2 Group Mitchell fitted with British-type flash suppressors. W/O Fenwick flew 50 operations in Mitchells, according to the original caption to this photograph. *IWM*

the bombers in a box all the while the boxes in the formation were close enough to give covering fire to one another. All aircraft would be corkscrewing and the box itself be turning into the attack. Suddenly, on a word of command from the gunnery controller in the lead Mitchell, all evasive action would cease and a minimum of 12×.50in machine guns would open fire on the attacking fighter(s). The fighter would have to break off as the only way he would get through would be to shoot a Mitchell out of the way or collide with one.

'The only time fighters were a danger to a well-controlled Mitchell force was if a tail-end man straggled and fell behind. A good lead crew would never let that happen even slowing down the force to enable the straggler to stay in position. Several times my own skipper allocated his aircraft to a new crew who he felt would not be able to get the best out of the aircraft whilst he took over the older and probably slower aircraft to lead the formation.

'The Wright Cyclone engines of the Mitchell were very reliable and it was not difficult to hold speed and altitude on one engine. Many an aircraft came back with big holes in the wing, tail, fins or fuselage and I was in one Mitchell that took a full salvo of four 88mm flak shells and lost part of the tail, the starboard engine and a couple of the bottom pots in the port engine, as well as having a lot of holes in the fuselage. We dropped like a stone until I was able to jettison the bombs and my skipper sorted out the fuel and power problems. We were then able to maintain a reasonable height and get it down on its wheels at the far end of the runway at West Malling in Kent. That aircraft was flying again in three months.

'Every crew practised single-engined flying and the main problem was lifting the wing again if you had to turn into the dead engine. The lift had to be entirely on aileron and rudder, as if you attempted to use engine, you were liable to go right over on to your back. There was another problem: although I'm not exactly certain about this, I believe that the main alternator was incorporated into the starboard engine and if you lost that you lost most of your services. I can't remember all the details but I know when we lost the starboard engine I lost control of the bomb doors and bombing circuits and had to use the manual jettison lever; I believe I had to pump down the wheels and flaps.

'In the earlier model B-25C/D, we had a problem with hydraulics, which would occasionally seize up, making it impossible to pump either wheels or flaps down against the pressure build-up. If this happened and a wheels up landing had to be made, the under (dustbin) turret could be pushed up from the bottom causing the whole structure, plus the upper turret, to be pushed forward. This broke the back of the aircraft, as the whole upper turret structure was forced down on to the W/Op's position. Apparently there was no way of forseeing when this would happen, or what in fact caused the hydraulics to seize up, until one of the groundcrew flight sergeants of No 226 came up with a theory. (I am not sure now whether it was F/Sgt Lofty Dalton of B Flight or F/Sgt White of A Flight who had the brainwave, but it was certainly "Chalky" White who told my skipper and me all about it.)

'On the B-25, the bomb doors, flaps, undercarriage, dustbin turret and brakes were hydraulically operated from the same reservoir and pumps and controlled by a five-way valve on which there were leather washers. The theory was that after an intermediate period of time, the washers absorbed hydraulic fluid and became pulpy and oversized. The operation of a major system such as the turret raise/lower or closing the bomb doors would put high positive pressure on the valve, which would stick. Pressure would be too high for the manual hand pump to be operated to lower the flaps and undercarriage — that was the theory, although the Accident Investigation Board was unable to prove it at that time because when the washer was examined it had dried out and was in fact undersized.

'About this time, Chalky White told us that he reckoned our aircraft was about due for hydraulic trouble, and should we find that the flaps and undercarriage would not lower, we should call the controller over the R/T and get him into the tower. He then showed me one of the hydraulic pipes and told me that if we had trouble lowering the flaps and gear, I should cut this pipe, drain that part of the system and then pump down the undercart. Needless to say, we had no problem for a couple of trips — and then it happened, no flaps, or gear. I tried pumping and bent the handle but could not get any response. Eventually I cut the pipe, got everything soaked in fluid, but was then able to pump down the wheels and we landed safely. Chalky removed the washers from the valve and put them into a jar of fluid for later examination. Sure enough, they were pulpy and swollen. From then on, the washers were changed at every major inspection and we never had any more trouble with hydraulics.

'After September 1944, being on a Mitchell squadron was a good life; the multi-sorties of the early days just before and after the invasion had ceased and crews were rarely called upon to do more than one sortie a day — lead crews got much less than even that — and the opposition was sparse. Unless we had a major target such as Bocholdt, Dortmund, Kleve or the Rhine bridges, the flak was practically non-existent. Fighters were conspicious by their absence and from January 1945 until the end of the war, I never saw one, except for one occasion in April when a Me262 climbed up through the formation while we were bombing Bochum. It went up like a bat out of hell and disappeared, apparently en route for the moon. No-one really saw what it was — it may even have been an Me 163 rocket fighter — but whatever it was, it did no harm to the formation.

'The Mitchell squadrons were heavily involved in Arnhem, the Rhine crossing and the Ardennes breakout, during which No 226 flew many sorties, but to the best of my knowledge, we only operated in single box formations, as we were then bombing only a few hundred yards in front of our own troops. This was also the only period when our squadrons operated on Christmas Day.

'Apart from one or two notable exceptions, such as Deventer Bridge, the targets were easy and, from about February 1945, we started to get a lot of passengers. The training units were closing down and the word was around that there was no sense in applying for a permanent commission unless you had at least some operational experience. We therefore had a big influx of instructors to fly with us. On one such sortie we had no less than four wing commanders and 13 squadron leaders following us!

'The Deventer Bridge effort was quite a story: three times we had attacked it but had only inflicted superficial damage and the flak was building up and getting very accurate — the count was 47 guns, plus light flak guarding the bridge. Finally the word came that the bridge had to go, come what may and we drew the lead position for the wing. It was to be a two wing effort, but each box was to bomb individually. Unfortunately, my skipper broke his arm (he fell off the mantlepiece when playing his bagpipes) and we had to hand over to Wg Cdr Wood, our squadron commander. His navigator also went sick and my skipper offered the CO my services. I was not that keen, as the CO had passed through my hands while I was instructing at No 2 GpSU. He was a very good pilot but did not take kindly to being told what evasive action to take by his crew. However, everything went well and he held the wing together very well until we reached the target area. No 139 wing was ahead of us and we could see the reception it was getting. It was warm, to say the least — 47 guns can put up quite a show when they are defending a target as small as a bridge and they can see the formations of bombers queuing up to start their attack.

'The CO would not take any notice of the evasive action I was calling for. (Both my brothers were Ack Ack officers and I carried a stop-watch, a list of probable prediction times, times of flight, etc. My skipper and I had worked out a plan of gentle evasive action which allowed him to keep the formations together and which encouraged the flak gunners to continue to predict, rather than go for a box barrage. It was always an exciting trip but we never had an aircraft in any formation we led seriously damaged by flak.) With this CO we did no evasive action until the flak gunners had got us well predicted — and then he threw the formation all over the sky. Apart from making it really hard work

148
A Mitchell II of No 320
(Netherlands) Squadron after a
forced landing at Eindhoven
following attention by
Fw190s. *via R. L. Ward*

for the other crews to stay in a tight box to give me a good bomb pattern, he toppled the gyros in my bombsight sighting head, got baulked by one of the No 320 Squadron formations breaking away, flew us straight into the flak being put up against No 139 Wing and got us right out of position. Eventually we attacked in a steep diving turn with the bombsight sighting plate rocking like a see-saw and the rest of the box trying hard to keep position. When the photographs were developed, it showed that all the other formations had narrowly missed the bridge because of what was obviously a wind error, whereas we had well and truly clobbered the northern approach and had taken out the northern span! The wing commander got a DFC whilst I got a roistering from the rest of the squadron for leading them in that chaotic manner and a remark from my skipper as to why the hell I couldn't do the same when he was flying!

'Decorations were very hard to come by in 2 Group and especially for the Mitchell squadrons. All the time I was with No 226, I think there were less than a dozen all together. My own skipper got a DFC at the end of the war, as did the other flight commander and, I think, one other pilot. Sqn

Ldr Lyle was awarded his DFC after he had completed his third tour of ops on Blenheims, Bostons and Mitchells and his navigator, Flt Lt Thomas, got his after completing 105 operations. His was the only case that I knew of a navigator getting a decoration — in fact the squadrons were told not to make recommendations for any aircrew, other than pilots, who had less than 100 operations.

'Formation flying was always a speciality of the 2 Group squadrons, no matter whether the aircraft was the Blenheim, Boston, Mosquito or Mitchell. For low level operations, the formation was a pair (normally spaced at four minute intervals — which we always thought was set so that German gunners would have a chance to disengage from one pair as it went out of range and swing round to engage the next two) whereas the medium level attack was by basically a "box" of six aircraft, made up of two 'vics" of three. On a low level approach, the rear vic would pull out and fly in echelon, closing up into the box when the climb to bombing altitude was started. Within the vic, the wingmen flew above the leader, but once in the box, the leader of the second vic dropped down and his wingman dropped down below him. This kept everyone out of the slipstream and allowed a good, tight formation to be maintained.

'After the fiasco of the first ''Circus'' in Mitchells, it was obvious that there would have to be a change of tactics and alterations made to our formation flying and escort operations. It had been the practice for a small force of fighters (two pairs) to act as close escort and stay with the bombers right on the bomb run and the rest of the escort to stay high and up-sun of the bombers. On the break-away, the bombers belted for home at low level and left the fighters to cover their retreat. Now it was seen that the Mitchells would have to gain height much earlier, the pick-up by the German radar would be much earlier and the defences would be alerted that much sooner. Apart from the extra flak that could be expected, enemy fighters could be airborne and well positioned for a full scale attack. This meant that RAF formations must be better co-ordinated one with another and with the larger fighter escort that would be needed.

'As a first stage, No 226 was taken out of the line and some of its lead crews sent, with their aircraft, to the Day Fighter Leaders' School to evolve and discuss tactics. After about a month at Aston Down, we then moved with the rest of the squadron to Drem in Scotland to practice

these new tactics of medium level approach and attack, mutual defence between boxes and co-ordinated defence with escorting fighters.

'We soon came to the conclusion that we needed to fly a very tight formation if it was to be operated as one unit. We tried the USAAF ''Nine Formation'' but rejected it as unwieldy and reverted to our box of six. We decided that the box should be set up as quickly as possible after take off, and stay tight until the top of the climb, which was ideally 500ft per minute, as soon as we left the circuit. During the approach to the enemy coast, the box could loosen up a bit, but should never be greater than one wingspan between aircraft. Over enemy territory and especially over the target area, the formation should be really tight. There could be violent manoeuvres but with a very tight formation, evasive action, both for flak and fighters could be sufficient.

'Evasive action for fighters was: leader and No 4 snaking in the vertical plane, Nos 2 and 3 corkscrewing outwards and Nos 5 and 6 corkscrewing inwards, while the whole box took a gentle but steady turn into the attack. On the command from the gunnery controller (usually in the lead aircraft), the whole formation would steady up, close right in and bring all guns to bear. Other boxes in the formation would do

149
Century Note: The 100th bomb symbol, in appropriately larger size than the rest, is applied to the nose of *Grumpy*, believed to have been FL176/B of No 98 Squadron. If so, the aircraft was the 2 Group Mitchell sortie record holder with 125 bombing operations and three ASR patrols. The records are not clear on how many others reached the 100 ops mark, but it is thought that there were no more than three in total. At least a dozen flew well over 50. *Bruce Robertson*

149

likewise to give mutual protection against co-ordinated attacks from more than one direction. The fighter escort would keep outside the gun range of the Mitchells, attack any fighters approaching the bombers and take them as they broke away. (I flew as a passenger in a Beaufighter making a simulated attack on a four-box formation of Mitchells and I have never been so scared, either before or since — and they were not firing either!)

'We gradually gave up our fighter close escort and escort cover force and opted for top, target and return cover. These were i) a small force of fighters flying high and in front on the approach to the enemy coast; ii) a medium level force in the target area to keep enemy fighters from interfering with the bombing run, and iii) a small fighter force at our own level or slightly higher to protect our tails on the way home. Eventually, even this escort was dispensed with and if we had any at all, it was usually a fighter sweep over the target before and just after we attacked. Sometimes in the days after D-Day, with Bomber Command operating in force by day; both US 8th and 9th Air Forces; fighters and fighter bombers of Nos 83 and 84 Groups, Fighter Command; Coastal Command and Fleet Air Arm Seafires, it was hard to find any space to fly in, let alone try any sophisticated defensive tactics! We had VHF communications with our fighter escort, but were not normally on a common frequency with fighters and the GCI controllers.

'As No 226 had carried out all the trials with the DFLS and 13 Group squadrons at Drem, its formation flying was much tighter than that of other Mitchell squadrons; whereas the others used to fly about half a wingspan between wingtips, we flew with our wings overlapping and with the No 4 man with his nose right under the leader's tail, the vertical separation between adjacent aircraft being less than ten feet. This could be very frightening for a new navigator sitting in the bomb-aiming position of the No 5 or 6 aircraft, looking up to see the bomb doors of the aircraft in front opening up less than ten feet above and only a few feet in front of him. When the bombs began to fall, there were very few who would not admit to calling on their Maker. Once you realised that the bombs would not hit you, it gave you quite a thrill.

'To see our squadron take off was quite a sight, too. At Swanton Morley, which was a grass airfield, we took 12 aircraft off in echelon starboard — wonderful towards the west, but a little dicey towards the east. The tower was to the south of the field and if the leader was slightly off course as he began rolling, it meant that No 12 would be pushed towards it. As there was a big bump in the middle of the airfield, it could be a bit hairy coming over the hill in the No 12 position to find the tower in your way. Ours was certainly not the only crew to take off on occasion between the tower and the hangars.

'Once we started to operate from runways, we kept to this fast take off technique and it was quite a sight to see 12 or even 18 Mitchells rolling together. We would take off — and land — faster than many fighter squadrons and I have seen a

150
Invasion-striped Mitchell IIs of No 320 Squadron on the bomb line at Melsbroek, Belgium, winter 1944. *IWM*

whole wing of 54 Mitchells and Bostons break over base, go into a long line astern and land in stream. The last aircraft touched down before the first had turned into dispersal.

'Two anecdotes regarding formation flying in Mitchells highlight the points made. When we were at Drem our CO was Wing Commander ''Charlie'' Tait (brother of the No 617 Sqdn CO). One day he led a vic of three Mitchells with Flt Lt (later Sqn Ldr) ''Paddy'' Lyle as No 2 and our own crew with F/Sgt ''Hank'' Storey, RCAF, as skipper of the No 3 aircraft. In accordance with briefing, the sortie was flown in complete R/T silence (in fact I cannot recall if we had been fitted with VHF at that time) and after about half an hour's fighter affiliation, the fighter boys went home. We stayed at 10,000ft. I then saw that Tait had both hands off the pole and was apparently beckoning us in closer. Paddy Lyle apparently thought so too, as he edged in as well. Hank could not see the leader, so he closed in on Paddy. Still the CO called us in. He started to dive like the clappers and was shaking his fists and still calling us in, holding his arms out at the sides and bending them at the elbows, bringing his hands in and then out again. We followed him down and edged in even closer. There followed a really hairy trip through the Scottish glens at about 50ft, with a formation so close that our engines were level with the leader's wingtips and our wingtips level with his mid-upper turret — and all the time Charlie Tait was calling us in closer. Finally as we neared the Firth of Forth, he waved us into echelon and we came into land. As we got out of the aircraft we were met by a very irate Wingco, who screamed at us that ''the next time I signal you to widen out, you will do as you are bloody well told and do it at once.'' Apparently we had misinterpreted his arm signals and he had dived to get out of danger. He threatened to have us posted to night bombers but later saw the funny side — and from then on, whenever he led, we were his Nos 2 and 3.

'The second incident concerns another crew, operating from Hartford Bridge (later Blackbushe). They were a new crew and were flying the No 3 position at the time. The wing had returned from an operation over France and brought their bombs back, the target having been obscured by cloud. As the formation joined the circut, No 3 in the second box of No 226 started to overshoot on the inside of a turn. With the throttles right back and the undercarriage horn blaring, the navigator remembered hearing some of us older navs saying that when caught in similar circumstances they had opened the bomb doors quickly and closed them again, the air brake action of the doors slowing them sufficiently to allow them to maintain station. This he did and was pleased to see that he got the desired result.

'After the aircraft had landed, the armourers found that two bombs were missing, but confirmed that they had gone down ''safe'' with the fuzing links still in position. The squadron assumed that the bombs had gone down on the target when the abortive bomb run was made, but half an hour later, the telephones were red hot and there followed a visit by a very angry army colonel. It transpired that when the navigator had opened the doors, he had gone straight through the two-stage control, past the ''Open-safe'' position, into the ''Open-free'' position. As he had not waited the necessary 15 seconds in the ''Safe'' position, there had been a surge of power through the torpedo release and the circuits were operated. We carried our first two bombs on stations 1a and 2a, which were inter-connected with the torpedo release and the two bombs went. They had fallen on to an army camp near Hartford Bridge, bounced between the parade commander and his troops, gone over the top and finally skidded to a halt just under the adjutant's office window. Apparently the parade had broken up and scattered without the necessary command and the CO was, understandably, most annoyed. It cost the squadron a party for the army officers and a terse order from 2 Group HQ that the practice of using bomb doors as air brakes was to cease forthwith.

'Formation flying was very strenuous for a pilot and many a time I saw my pilot absolutely wet through from exertion. On a couple of occasions after a really hot time over the target when we led the wing, I went back through the tunnel to find that he had switched on the autopilot as soon as we had cleared enemy territory and gone to sleep — with a wing of aircraft formating on him! We used to pull his leg that the best formation was when he was asleep and ''George'' was leading.

'Although the Mitchell was used in all war theatres, it is doubtful if it could be cited as a successful weapon. It had neither the range nor load-carrying capacity of the Lancaster and Halifax, the speed or manoeuvrability of the Boston, Marauder or Invader, nor the speed, versatility or capacity of the Mosquito and without a doubt, had 2 Group been able to get sufficient Mosquitos, we would have dropped both the Mitchell and Boston before D-Day. As things were, the Mitchell served a very useful role and certainly so

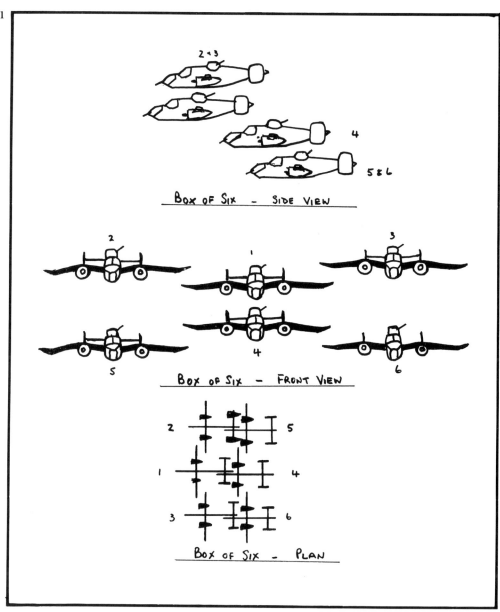

2 + 3

5 & 6

BOX OF SIX - SIDE VIEW

BOX OF SIX - FRONT VIEW

BOX OF SIX - PLAN

151
Diagram showing the tight
formation adopted by a box of
six 2 Group Mitchells, both for
effective fighter defence and a
concentrated bomb pattern.

in the phase August 1943 to August 1944 — the flying bomb and communications centre period — when the squadrons equipped with it more than held their own. The loss rate was extremely low and without a doubt, I and many more like me would not have survived the war had we not converted on to Mitchells. However, sometime in 1953, I read an Operational Research Branch analysis that stated that Mitchells needed to drop nearly ten times as many bombs as Mosquitos to get a hit on a small target such as a bridge, and that fighter bombers with rockets or bombs were more than five times more effective than Mosquitos. I did not entirely agree with these findings, as they were loaded against the Mitchell.

'Considering that we operated six aircraft as one unit and bombing as one, it meant that on every run we released 24 bombs, all of which were likely to go astray if the wind vector had been incorrectly calculated. The Mosquito on the other hand, operated singly from zero feet, thus eliminating all wind errors. A squadron of 12 Mitchells would at best have two tries under better conditions and drop 48 bombs, whereas 12 Mosquitos would have 12 tries under better conditions and drop 24 bombs. They had the advantage of dropping at low level, when as we knew from Boston and Blenheim experience, every bomb dropped hit the target. The fighter bombers were even better off as rockets had as much destructive power as our bombs and these aircraft could each make three or four runs on the target to our one for every six aircraft. Taking these factors into consideration, the Mitchells were bound to compare unfavourably as a cost effective weapon. However, I like them and will always remember them with great affection.'

Stoney's Story John Stone

Lt John William Stone's first combat mission took place on 3 November 1944 when he was a new first pilot in the 501st Bomb Squadron of the 345th Group. Interestingly enough, 'Stoney' had graduated from high school in 1940 at Tampa, Florida, where the school mascot was the Black Panther. When he arrived at the squadron HQ he found that the Intelligence Officer was Capt Benjamin Green, who had been a band director at the school, 'Stoney' having been head cheerleader:

'Imagine that: a pilot arriving in the jungles of New Guinea all the way from Florida to find a person he was closely allied to in high school already there and the mascot of his assigned squadron being the same as it was in school. Quite a coincidence.

'The anticipation and anxiety of a pilot's first combat mission can perhaps be likened to the honeymoon night; the first day of high school; the first date when driving the family car for the first time — and more importantly the first time that somewhere in your life you have faced a fight where you had to attack in order to preserve your life, your masculinity, your position, or your status with your teenage girl friend. Of capital importance; the first mission is that point in life when death is faced for the first time; yet you are willing to do so because it is for the benefit of your country and you have this deep inner feeling that your cause is a noble one and that you are there on a mission meaningful for everyone you love.

'After having delivered a new B-25 from the States to Townsville, I was assigned to a training command at Nadzab and introduced to jungle airstrips, a style of flying that was so different from that in Air Training Command, and experienced veterans who had a certain nonchalance about them that was indefinable, indistinguishable from reality and undecipherable as to just what was their attitude toward life now that they had been in combat, completed their missions and were assigned to teaching the new men how to get along up there. So, after the usual combat training in an actual combat area and flying the usual training mission to Wewak, I was assigned to the 501st on Biak Island at the western end of the Netherlands East Indies.

'On 2 November I flew as a co-pilot to Morotai, landing there late in the evening where the scenario was to spend the night and take off early the next morning to hit the township of Alicante, on Negros in the Philippines. The first item of significance was that as yours truly and his crew were being transported over rain infested muddy roads to a transit camp for the overnight sleeping experience, one of the trucks signalled a red alert. Three great booms in sequence from some large anti-aircraft gun warned everyone about an enemy air attack.

'As my truck moved along, a Japanese white phosphorous bomb exploded, causing the entire jungle landscape to light up as if it were midday. The truck continued to move but at the next opportunity after more bombs had been dropped, the entire complement bailed out and ran off the road into the shelter of trees. I ran for some two or three hundred yards, hearing the explosions of bombs and trying to escape the holocaust if one came close to me or the trucks on the road.

'A short time later a Japanese reconnaissance plane dropped another bomb and illuminated the area where I had hidden. I was in the middle of a bomb dump. Had phosphorous landed in my area and splashed any bombs, it would have immediately burned through their casing and probably obliterated the new crew members on the spot.

'When the all-clear sounded, all of us due for the mission reached the transit camp and found accommodation in tents. In almost all cases the tents were leaning and the legs of the cots sinking down into the floors, which were 100 per cent mud.

'Well before daybreak on 3 November, 48 B-25s of the 345th Group, comprising 12 planes from each of the four squadrons, convened on the steel mat and prepared for take off. The planes were mired in mud and in many cases it took the firing up of the engines to maximum rpm to extricate them; others had to be moved out by ground equipment to get them on to the runway. The ordnance people had loaded each B-25J with the maximum amount of 50-cal ammunition for the 14 forward firing guns, as well as 500lb on some and parafrags on others. Once the engines were started, all planes were basically in order in the jungle darkness and proceeded to the take off position.

152
Apache Hunting Party: Two dozen B-25Js of all four squadrons of the 345th flying over the South China Sea early in 1945. Under the command of group CO Col Chester A. Coltharp, the mission was a search for a reported Japanese convoy.
USAF via Frank F. Smith

'Even though I came over as first pilot, I was assigned as co-pilot to the plane that was to fly on the right wing of the squadron leader. Four flights of three planes would later manoeuvre themselves into two flights of six abreast — six bombing and strafing followed by another six for a total of 48, blanketing the target to the point that the airfield should cease to function in defence of our invasion of the Philippines.

'All engines were running and planes were advancing one by one, creeping along to get into take off position, Jeeps and other forms of transportation were running back and forth with dimmed lights as ground personnel organised last minute preparations for this important mission. As my plane approached the take off point, a Jeep roared up with a passenger waving in

dramatic fashion. This was interpreted to mean that I should respond. The passenger was Capt Hilding Jacobsen (now a retired Major General) who jumped from the Jeep signalling that the B-25's entrance ladder should be released. The flight engineer complied and Capt Jacobsen climbed up enough to state in a very loud voice over the very loud noise of the engines that Lt Stone remove himself and get into another plane. Lt Stone complied; unbuckled from the seat and went down the ladder whereupon the Captain instructed him to take the co-pilot's seat in the lead plane. Capt Jacobsen had been to the lead plane and extracted a Lt Waldo to take my place. I was going to co-pilot the 501st Squadron lead ship, while Lt Waldo, also a newcomer who had arrived about the same time as me, would fly the wing. That decision was to be very consequential to the lives of Lt Stone, who was single and Lt Waldo, who was married.

'The mission took off into the darkness, the aircraft creating the weird sounds tyres make against steel matting, and climbed with formation navigation lights on. We maintained a loose formation until daybreak as this was a long flight and we were relatively safe until the sun came up. Then the formation became tighter and tighter.

'Despite the last minute change of aircraft, it was reassuring for me to be in the lead plane, as I could observe the skills of the first pilot, which could auger well for my future combat career. Slowly time moved to the target approach. Many thoughts go through the mind of a pilot at this point, among them death and the consequences of death upon those he would leave behind. Although I was unmarried, I had a very close relationship with my mother, who was particularly dependent on me, and a brother who was then in the army.

'The weather en route to the target was excellent and the formation was straight out of flying school, everyone in proper shape, and feeling that the equipment was in good order and the ordnance adequate for the mission. Alicante airfield was a grass strip with earth embankments protecting the fighters against bombing raids and our plan was to approach from west to east over the northern tip of the island; opposition was expected to be Zero fighters as well as very effective 20mm anti-aircraft fire from emplacements which the Japanese had learned to deploy so effectively around their airfields. We flew to the target at about 2,500ft, but descended to about 200ft over enemy territory.

'As attack time approached, the entire group of 48 planes climbed to about 500ft in order to dive and accumulate speed. I was excited, knowing that my main responsibility was to be aware of what went on and keep the airplane from flying into the ground or any other B-25. I also had to snap on the cameras which took pictures from the rear of the aircraft to show the effects of the mission and of course, to always be in a position to take over the first pilot's duties in the event he became incapacitated.

'As the ascent to the predive on the target proceeded, flak helmet and vest were checked, as well as the seat belt. All crew members were called in to be sure they knew we were going in; all answers

153
It had taken the Falcons a lot of hard fighting to get as far as Okinawa in July 1945, where this B-25J was photographed. The striking red and yellow nose marking is shown to advantage. *Frank F. Smith*

were positive and we headed in, the lead plane of the element. Lt Waldo's plane was on my right wing.

'Each Mitchell unleashed its 14 forward firing guns and we pulverised the airfield as the Japanese responded with AA fire, which we could easily see. As we were committed to our dive, I made sure that I was the proper distance from my wingman. Suddenly I saw him take hits in the left nacelle. The aircraft lurched forward and in toward mine. I grabbed the co-pilot's control column and pulled us up to avoid the other plane colliding with us. Fortunately, the right hand plane regained control and moved into position again, but fire was visible streaming back from that left engine. Suddenly the left wheel dropped and the fire erupted, engulfing the wing, which split off from the fuselage. The plane immediately corkscrewed down, hit the ground and exploded. There could not possibly have been any survivors.

'Shocked by the loss of that particular aircraft, I wondered again at the decision to switch co-pilots, because that could so easily have been me. We made a high speed dash off the target, my very skilled pilot staying as close to the ground as he possibly could. Out over the water with the propeller tips only inches from the surface, we actually left a wake. With engine cylinder head temperatures almost on the red line, the ''Air Apaches'' flew out to sea, rejoined and headed back to Morotai to refuel.

'The trip back was uneventful, except

for the feelings that go with the loss of your comrades as you survey the effect of the mission. The 3 November mission ended later that day, with the planes refuelling. They took off for their main base on Biak to be immediately rearmed and refuelled again for another Philippine mission the following day.

'I could not forget how I had been spared, or stop wondering why — why was Lt Waldo taken from the plane that was not shot down? Why was he the one to go in? Is something like that attributable to God? Luck? Was there a plan by an omnipotent force that said Lt Waldo had served his purpose on earth and that Lt Stone had not yet received the chance to serve his? Is it religious? Why? Probably every person who has flown in combat and seen his comrades fall wonders why he was not the one and why he survived. And I am sure that many of those, as they were falling, wondered why it had to be they who were chosen to become the fallen angel.'

John Stone went on to fly 17 more missions in the South West Pacific, logging 104 hours, 55 minutes combat time with the 'Air Apaches' before an old B-25 in which he was a passenger crashed on its way back to the war zone from New Guinea. After being treated for burns, he was given the option of more combat flying or going home — he chose the latter. His last combat mission was to bomb and strafe targets on Luzon on 8 February 1945.

154
When the 345th returned home in December 1945, some squadron aircraft apparently staged through India. This unarmed 500th BS machine was one of them. Zero length rocket launchers were fitted in time for use in the last months of the war. *Bruce Robertson*

Solid Truck

Hans van der Kop

'Mitchell crews of No 320 (Dutch) Squadron were made up as those in other RAF units flying the aircraft — one pilot, one navigator (observer/bombardier) and two gunners — until G-H bombing through cloud was introduced. Then the lead aircraft generally carried an extra navigator. The squadron operated with a strength of around 18 to 20 aircraft and about 26 to 28 crews. In the latter part of the war, these consisted not only of Dutchmen but British, Commonwealth and Belgian airmen.

'The Mitchell was a formidable aircraft in combat, that is to say it could take quite a beating from anti-aircraft fire and still get home. On one occasion, a No 320 Sqn aircraft had a rudder completely torn away when bombs from another formation went through ours; the aircraft remained controllable right until after landing. Another Mitchell came home after suffering a pierced main spar and other severe damage.

'The squadron rarely encountered enemy fighters, but many of the crews had doubts that the Mitchell's armament was sufficient to withstand fighter attack. For that reason, we developed the practice of corkscrewing in formation, worked out during fighter affiliation flights. It was a very unhealthy manoeuvre, but the best one we had.

'My first operation was very nearly my last. We were shot up over the Pas de Calais after bombing a V-weapons target; one engine went out but the propeller could not be feathered as the hydraulics had been damaged. With full power on the other engine, the aircraft was brought

155

155
Sub-Lt Hans van der Kop (extreme right) with members of his crew. To his immediate left is Cdr Burgerhout, who flew more than 72 sorties with No 230 and led the squadron as CO from 1944, being awarded the British DSO and the Military Willems Order, the Dutch equivalent of the Victoria Cross. On Cdr Burgerhout's left is senior squadron gunner Van Lingen (83 2 Group ops) and finally, second gunner Goudeketting (65 Mitchell operations). The use of surnames only was common in the Dutch services and crews were often identified by the name of the pilot — 'crew Burgerhout' and so on. *Hans van der Kop*

156
Dutch personnel return General Eisenhower's salute during a 'top brass' visit to Dunsfold in May 1944. Air and ground crews of No 320 Squadron were composed mainly of men of the Royal Netherlands Naval Air Service and the military aviation branch of the Dutch Army and although operational aircrew wore standard RAF issue uniforms, NCOs wore forage caps with Dutch titlings. *IWM*

157, 158
National pride was reflected on RAF aircraft flown by Dutchmen both in nose art and the black-bordered orange triangle, a modified form of the 'Neutrality' marking first used in 1914.
Both Royal Netherlands Navy

159
Crews attend to last-minute details as the bombs roll out to the Mitchells. In the foreground is FR165 which crashed after a collision with another Mitchell II (FW212) at Tirlemont on 9 February 1945.
Royal Netherlands Navy

back to Friston, a diversionary base near Eastbourne, where the undercarriage was lowered with the emergency system. After landing, emergency braking was used. Countless holes were noted, one piece of flak having gone through the bottom of the aircraft and finished up in the roof — right in the spot where I had stood a second before. That was the only operation I flew that resulted in an emergency diversion, but other crews had to bail out (some over enemy territory) or ditch.

'The toughest targets were the V sites in the Pas de Calais, as were the bridges in Holland or the heavily-defended harbours of Brest and Cherbourg. Providing support for the armies near Caen was also hard. On 23 October 1944, No 320 had a complete box scattered by flak over Brest, killing two crews and wounding many others. Evasive action, even during the bombing run, was necessary to give us more chance. Later in the war, the Germans used to put up barrage flak, as well as aimed fire, which made evasive action difficult.

'Fighter protection was always generous. Sometimes 12 Mitchells were sent out over Europe to be bait for German fighters, with six to ten squadrons of Allied fighters as escort. As soon as the flak came up, the close escort moved away a bit . . .

'Abandoning the Mitchell was easy for the gunners in the rear and the pilot, but if the navigator was in the nose, his chances were small and for that reason, he used to sit in the second pilot's seat as soon as bombing was over. That was also his emergency station — if he could make it through the tunnel that ran from the navigator's compartment to the nose.

'Servicing the Mitchell was not difficult, as it came with sound American philosophy towards such things. Liaison with the technical branch of the squadron was close and for a long time, a Dutch system was used whereby each aircraft had a ''paai'', a technician who was responsible for ''his'' aircraft. Communication between the groundcrews and flying crews was therefore established and also encouraged by both the squadron commander and the head of the technical branch. For operational reasons in 2 TAF, No 6320 Servicing Echelon was introduced, a unit which was independent and had its own CO (ie the technical officer), but as we were a small unit of Dutchmen who knew each other very well, there were complaints about this new set up. Personally though, I preferred a groundcrew to be responsible to the squadron CO.

'The planning of missions was sometimes sketchy when the squadron first started operations, but improved immensely as photographic reconnaissance of targets improved. But boobs were still made. On 3 March 1945, No 320 was ordered to bomb the Hague in an attempt to destroy a V-2 store. Although many of the Dutch crews knew that the

target had no military value and said so, the operation went on. It was a disaster. Bombs, dropped hundreds of yards from the correct aiming point, flattened thousands of houses, killing and wounding more than 3,000 people. The raid became a political issue in later years and still stands as a black page in 2 Group's history.

'Night flying in formation was tried with Mitchells, but abandoned after a number of accidents. During the day, the increasing accuracy of German flak led to bombing runs being shortened when the Mk XIV bombsight became operational. The sight also allowed the aircraft to weave during the bombing run, but it also depended very much on wind conditions over the target. I was not alone in recommending the despatch of an aircraft to fly a ''wind pattern'' above our targets, just before the arrival of the main force. This procedure helped improve bombing accuracy, as otherwise one depended solely on met information. During bad weather in September 1944, a Gee climb-out procedure was introduced, allowing the aircraft to take-off in a steady stream and still form up quickly when above cloud.

'In the last stages of the war, No 320 Squadron received some Mk III Mitchells with tail guns. These aircraft were more gun platforms than bombing platforms and I personally found that they were less

steady on the bombing run, but they had more armour and could take more punishment. According to the pilots, their flying characteristics in the formation boxes was somewhat different. Technically they were also improved, the top turret being modified so that a large man could fit himself in.

'Although comparing the Mitchell with the Mosquito was like comparing a solid truck with a fast sports car, it came out well against other aircraft more in its class. From heresay, American crews regarded the Mitchell as dependable aircraft, even on one engine, whereas the Marauder was considered to be a killer when one engine seized; 9th USAAF crews had occasion to use our field in emergencies and what I saw made me doubt that I would have ever liked to fly the Marauder. Some US pilots who joined British squadrons on exchange said that they certainly preferred the Mitchell to the B-26.

'Regarding operations, my most lasting impression was that many people who hardly knew each other performed as a team, saw many of their number lost but carried on themselves, motivated by a desire to end the horrors of war, for which all of us must be held responsible. We felt that No 320 was as good a squadron as any.'

160
'Z-Zulu' was FR201, seen here in full D-day markings awaiting the next call to action while the crew relax for a precious few minutes. The aircraft survived the war and passed to the RNethAF in July 1947.
Royal Netherlands Navy

Mitchells Around the World

161

161
Palawan: Damage, possible as a result of a collision, suffered by a 42nd Group B-25J, 43-27958. The aircraft bears the grey shield and a red Cross of Lorraine 'Crusaders' badge adopted by the group late in 1944, plus the yellow tail tips. These markings were applied to the majority of C, G and J Mitchells operated by the 42nd's five squadrons.
Frank F. Smith

162
Admiralty Islands: B-25G 42-64947 and B-25J 43-27794 of the 42nd Bomb Group, 13th Air Force, en route to Hollandia from the Russell and Treasury Islands for 10 days operations with the A-20s of the 312th Group in western New Guinea. Thereafter, the B-25s of the Crusaders moved on, to Sansapor on the Vogelkopf pensinsula of New Guinea. The group finally ended up at Palawan and flew sorties in support of the Philippines campaign. *USAF*

162

163
England: A B-25J (44-29125) reportedly assigned to the 25th Bomb Group (Reconnaissance), 8th Air Force, landing at Watton in 1945. The records show that the group returned to the USA during July-August, although the 'buzz number' BD-125 carried by this aircraft was not authorised until November 1945 — perhaps this Mitchell was left behind? *via Paul Coggan*

164
Brazil: Belem was an early staging point on the southern ferry route for US aircraft destined for European combat units. Nearest the camera in this line-up is a B-25C in 'desert pink' camouflage while an olive drab example is one B-24D and B-26 down the row. *IWM*

165
Aleutian Islands: Landing on
the runway at Elexai Point,
Attu, on 13 November 1943,
this B-25G skidded on the
snow-brushed steel mat, cut
into the tail of another B-25
taxying for take off and slid off
the north end of the runway
into rock hard earth. The
sliding Mitchell passed within
yards of two 343rd FG P-40s,
to end up merely as a source of
spares. *USAF*

166
Alaska: Ladd Field at 35°
below was no place to hang
around a flightline for engines
to warm up. Leaving portable
heaters to do the job on these
28th Composite Group B-25Cs,
the groundcrews have retired
to shelter and warmth. *USAF*

167
Australia: The only Mitchell
Squadron composed of
Australian personnel was
No 2, although No 18
(Netherlands East Indies)
operated under RAAF control.
No 2 withdrew from
operations in May 1944,
relinquishing Beauforts and
carried out its first offensive
sorties with the new type on
27 June, nine aircraft being
provided for a strike on Timor.
Operating with No 18, No 2
Sqn was based at Hughes,
Northern Territory, where
these B-25D and J models
were photographed in July
1945. *via Frank F. Smith*

168
Australia: Typical of No 2
Sqn's Mitchells was this
camouflaged J model, A47-31/
KO-P, photographed at Hughes
in 1944. The squadron also
flew natural metal finish
aircraft, operating a mixture
of early and late models
throughout its Mitchell
period. *Frank F. Smith*

168

We Missed Bodenplatte
Malcolm Scott

'My first sight of a B-25 Mitchell was in May 1943, at Dum Dum airfield, Calcutta. My squadron, No 34 (Bomber) in 221 Group, was on its way south from Assam, our general operational duties in support of the 14th Army in Burma having been taken over by Vengeances and Hurribombers. For the last 18 months, I had been on Blenheim IVs and, in the final stages, Blenheim Vs which we, in our ignorance, called Bisleys.

'The leggy appearance of the B-25 on its tricycle undercarriage was intriguing and, as it took off, the healthy roar of the Wright Cyclone engines sounded most impressive to aircrew who had been flying ''clapped out'' aircraft for so long. I had no idea at the time that little over a year later I was to renew my acquaintance with the Mitchell but on a much closer basis.

'I was repatriated in 1944, landing at Liverpool a few days before D-Day. A few weeks later, with the invasion successfully launched and V-1 ''doodlebugs'' buzzing in over the Kent coast on a reciprocal course, I was sent to Brackla, up in the north of Scotland, which was virtually a remuster-ing centre for operationally-expired aircrew. I was not at all happy at the thought of becoming an intelligence, transport or equipment officer, but my efforts to get back on ops for a second tour met with considerable resistance — until it was known that I had completed my first tour on daylight bombers as a leading navigator and bomb aimer. In next to no time, I was on my way south and arrived at No 13 OTU Bicester, where the station SP Flight Sergeant was the one who had looked me up and down so critically when I had reported there in 1941, with my shiny stripes and gleaming new brevet. This time, he saluted smartly and showed me the station adjutant's office.

'I had expected to go on Mosquito IVs — daylight bombers — which occupied Bicester, but I learnt that a few miles away at the satellite, Finmere, the CFI was Wing Commander T. A. Cox, my pilot in Burma, flying Mitchells. He was disenchanted with his current job and anxious to join an operational squadron. We quickly crewed up, sought out Flt Lt ''Stewy'' Needham, a W/Op air gunner who had been on No 34

169
Dunsfold Scene: Mitchell II FV916 of No 180 Squadron being fuelled and armed during Operation Starkey, in September 1943. An attempt to deceive the Germans that air operations were being stepped up prior to an invasion, it only achieved limited results. The aircraft shown had flown seven sorties by the time of the photograph and was used by the squadron from July 1943 to April 1944, when it was written off. *IWM*

Squadron with us, plus a gunnery leader, Flt Lt Ted Gill, who joined us to make up the full complement.

'Whilst the others were getting their grounding in their various categories during the first week or two of the course — not that the Wingco needed any — I spent a lot of time on Airspeed Oxfords and Ansons being introduced and trained on Gee, which I'd only heard of in the Far East. Having attained the necessary standard, we completed the rest of the OTU course as a crew and proceeded to 2 Group Support Unit, Swanton Morley. On our way there we saw the first wave of the paratroop assault droning out over the Norfolk coast towards Arnhem, although we were unaware of the target at the time.

'We worked up to a high standard of proficiency using the Mark XIV bombsight which was an enormous improvement on the Mk IX sight I had used previously. When the average error was down to 50 yards, we went on to night flying exercises, involving cross-country flights culminating in flare-dropping over a particular point at a particular time for the benefit of a Mosquito which it was intended, would identify suitable targets by the light of our flares.

'The weather during those few weeks in October was appalling; low cloud, heavy rain, mist and fog precluded the split-second navigation necessary and defeated any real chance of the idea working. On only one night did we have the satisfaction of hearing the Mossie tell us he was in the vicinity and could see our flares. We found the whole exercise fraught, frustrating and futile and we never had to repeat it after we left Swanton Morley.

'We received orders to join No 180 Squadron at Melsboek (Brussels) and arrived there on 10 December 1944. One flight to familiarise ourselves with the local geography and we were ready for the first operation of our second tour. This was on the 15th, to a road bridge at Zwolle, Holland, and the amount of flak thrown up at us was like nothing we had ever seen before. Then the weather closed right down on us and for a week we were grounded.

'It was during that week that the Germans started their totally unexpected offensive in the Ardennes and it was not until 22 December that we attempted a Gee-H attack on troop concentrations at Hinebach without seeing the results of our bombing, due to complete cloud cover over the target. The next day there was an attack on Schmidtheim; the bombing was accurate and concentrated — as was the flak!

'For the next three weeks, all our effort was flown into blasting the spearhead of the German attack, then on 1 January we were detailed to bomb a communications centre at Dasburg in Belgium. Leading us that day was No 320 Squadron and we circled the rendezvous point for ten minutes waiting for our fighter escort, which failed to show up. Radio silence was broken to ask control for instructions and a guarded response came back to say there would be no fighter escort and the decision would rest with the bombing leader. He announced, "We will press on." "In that case," cautioned control laconically, "watch out for fighters." Unbeknown to us of course, Operation Bodenplatte had been launched by the Luftwaffe that morning and our bases were under attack at the very time we were enquiring about our escort.

'The mission was accomplished successfully and on our return it was the one and only time when our ground crews, always keen to find out how we had fared on the "op" were instead bursting to tell us what it was like to be under a ground strafing attack. The few Mitchells we had left on the tarmac were write-offs and a dozen Wellingtons and Spitfires belonging to 34 PR Wing were no more than blazing hulks, with the smoke rising hundreds of feet into the air from the pyres.

'By the middle of January 1945 the German advance had been contained and we resorted to our more normal targets of oil refineries and dumps, troop concentrations, road and railway bridges and the inevitable marshalling yards. One such attack that I have good cause to remember took place on 11 March, a few days before my 24th birthday.

'We had been briefed at 08.00 for take-off at 10.25 to bomb the marshalling yards at Lengerich. There was a ground mist which cleared sufficiently for us to take-off on time and we formed up, leading the contingent of 34 Mitchells from 139 Wing and following the wing leader from No 226 Squadron of 137 Wing. We climbed through 10/10 strato-cumulus cloud with tops around 5,000ft and, as this was the longest penetration we had undertaken for some time, we would have preferred a greater height. Half an hour after we set course from Melsbroek, we picked up our fighter escort of Spitfires from Goch and altered course for our second turning point. We crossed the Rhine at Emmerich to be greeted with the usual heavy, accurate flak and flew on for another 40 minutes into Germany at 14,000ft, keeping in our defensive formation. Meanwhile, a thick layer of cloud began drifting in from the north, a

170
Invasion Garb: Mitchell II
FW124 of No 180 Squadron
bears evidence of wear and
tear during the immediate post
D-day period. Before the unit
moved to the continent in
September, EV-G went missing
during a sortie to Elbeuf on
21 August. *Frank F. Smith*

little above us as we neared the target. We dropped down to our bombing height of 12,000ft, breaking into our separate boxes and switched to our independent R/T bombing channels.

'Final checks on the bombsight were made to ensure that the last wind velocity and direction, calculated some eight minutes before, were correctly entered into the sight computer. Bomb fuses were switched to "live", the bomb spacing panel was set at 100ft intervals and the bomb release to "on". I told the pilot the target was in sight and as the flak began to burst around us, he started weaving along our course. I broadcast to my own particular box of aircraft, "Grey box, open bomb doors". Every bit of concentration was centred on getting the narrow neck of the marshalling yards ahead to run down the small glass panel of the bombsight towards the illuminated dagger. "Left, left" and the pilot kicked the port rudder pedal to follow my correction — as the bombing run was being broadcast, all the pilots in the box of six aircraft knew what manoeuvre to expect. "Steady" — flak was coming up thick and heavy, but at that moment only the air gunners were conscious of it, since they had nothing else to concentrate on. When flak appeared as black puffs in daylight it was not particularly worrying, but when it burst with red and orange centres — "hard" centres as our gunners called them — you clearly heard the crump, usually followed by the ping, ping as bits of shrapnel hit the aircraft, sometimes passing right through.

'The target slid down the blade of the dagger towards the cross hilt. "Ri-i-gh-t. — Steady." Another small correction by the pilot and the yards were within

seconds of receiving our visiting cards. The bomb run seemed like an age to the pilots and gunners, although it was never more than 20 seconds before I broadcast, to their relief, "Bombing". They knew at that moment that flying straight and level was nearly over and that the magic word "Go" would result in all six nav/bomb aimers pressing the bomb release tit at the same time and 48 500 pounders would start their irrevocable plunge to earth.

'As we started the bombing run, a train was approaching the marshalling yard. As I ordered "Bombing — bombing — bombing — go", the train drew into the immediate target area and its fate was sealed. By remarkable coincidence it was carrying ammunition — as the bombs struck home, the whole train blew up. I had watched the bombs from above falling at their usual trajectory — slowly and almost vertical at first, then appearing to level out the further they dropped away from the bomber, racing the aircraft above to the target below and finally disappearing for a few seconds before they exploded on impact. A great mushroom of flame surrounded by a black ring of blast came rushing up towards us, growing larger as it rose. An almighty "woomph" struck from underneath, rocking the aircraft violently and passed on heavenwards. A great pall of smoke and dust was rising as we turned for home, chased away by sporadic bursts of flak. We climbed up to 14,000ft again, to be joined by the Spits, which had risen high above us during the actual bombing.

'By then we were flying between two layers of cloud, alto-cumulus above and broken strato-cumulus below. We reached our first turning point, altered course on a very short leg and set course for Isselburg. Four miles south of Bocholt we encountered more flak and I had just pinpointed our position and worked out a new wind when Ted Gill come on the R/T, "Christ, look at this cheeky bastard." Not more than 20 yards away on our starboard beam was a grey and green camouflaged Bf109G. He had positioned himself slightly below our box where none of our gunners could bring their armament to bear and was looking over his shoulder at us and giving the V-sign.

'It was the old decoy trick and our fighter escort fell for it. They came roaring down from above and the '109 tipped on a wing and dived into the lower clouds with the Spitfires in hot pursuit. No sooner had the ''posse'' disappeared than we were jumped from behind. Out of the cloud above appeared a schwarm of four '109s with their cannon and machine guns blazing. Ted Gill, as gunnery leader, took over control. ''Bandits at four o'clock — turn to port — Go.'' We wheeled over, keeping tight formation, except for No 5, who was straggling somewhat. ''Bandits coming in eight o'clock — turn to starboard — Go.'' We turned into the attack and the cannon shells went whistling past, making long white spirals through the air, interspersed with tracer trails.

'It was now up to the pilots and air gunners. There was nothing the navigators could do but crouch down on their seats with a sheet of armour plate behind and hope for the best. I tried to concentrate on my navigation, keeping an eye on the map and the ground below, over which we kept

changing direction, ''They've got No 5'' yelled Stewy Needham. I peered down and behind to see the stricken Mitchell falling away from us with just a streak of smoke following him down. It looked as though the pilot had the aircraft under control, but tragically, he never pulled out of the dive. The Mitchell disintegrated as it struck the ground. No-one bailed out and the whole crew were killed.

'By then the Spitfires had realised what was going on and had regained their height, driving off the '109s but losing one of their number in the process.

'The cloud above us had now cleared, but there was still 8/10 fracto-cumulus below at 6,000ft. We reached the last turning point and turned for home. As we crossed the River Maas, I made a slight correction to our course and then left my compartment in the nose, hauled myself along the tunnel on my back to the pilot's cockpit and wearily took my place in the co-pilot's seat. The wingco glanced at me and grinned. ''Quite a trip, eh?.'' I felt drained. Having watched the results of one of the most accurate pieces of bombing I'd ever undertaken I had been elated up to the time of the fighter attack — now we'd lost one of our aircraft and crew. The running battle with the Bf109s had put us well behind the others and we circled base for nearly half and hour before landing.

'We were all glad to get debriefing over and we stood down for the rest of the day. Next morning it was business as usual. Another marshalling yard and the most flak we had ever encountered!'

171
Mitchell Mks II and III taxying out at Melsbroek, No 180 Squadron's last permanent wartime base. Between January and May 1945, the squadron virtually replaced its complement of Mk IIs with Mk IIIs — there were 18 Mk IIs and three Mk IIIs on hand in January, 19 Mk IIIs and only three Mk IIs by May, the three-squadron 139 Mitchell Wing then having 61 aircraft available. *IWM*

171

Zippers Over Kyushu

Eugene Olsen &
Warren Lovell

The 41st Bomb Group became the sole medium bomber element of the 7th Air Force when it was established at Hickam Field, Hawaii, on 16 October 1943. The 7th was about to undertake its first major offensive in the Central Pacific as part of Operation Galvanic, the assault on the Gilbert Islands. But it was not until late December, after the Gilberts had been secured, that the group's B-25s entered combat.

With airfields established on Tarawa, Abemama and Makin Atolls, Operation Flintlock was prepared to bring Kwajalein in the Marshall Islands, under US control. Accordingly, the 41st's 396th and 820th Squadrons based their B-25s on Tarawa, with the 47th and 48th on Abemama. The group went operational on 28 December 1943, the 820th BS flying the first mission, all squadrons having moved to the Gilberts during the period 17-24 December.

From January 1944, the 41st concentrated its attacks on Maloelap and Wotje as part of the Army-Navy softening up prior to the invasion of Kwajalein. Making good use of its B-25Gs, the group flew 215 ground attack sorties up to 12 February, for the loss of 17 aircraft — the Japanese had strong fighter forces in the Marshalls and seven B-25s were shot down. In an effort to reduce losses, the group switched to medium — up to 9,000ft — altitude bombing from 19 February, a move that had the desired effect. Japanese air strength was in any event ebbing and the Navy took Kwajelein early in February. Four atolls — Julait, Maloelap, Mille and Wotje — remained in enemy hands and were not invaded, the main American effort turning to Eniwetok, westernmost of the Marshalls atolls. It therefore fell to the 7th Air Force to contain what resistance there remained in the Marshalls, a task begun in February and lasting until April 1944. The 41st's B-25s flew well over 1,500 sorties in the first three months of the year and May saw the heaviest strike when 280 B-25s, B-24s, F4Us, SBDs and F6Fs dropped 240 tons of bombs on Juliat in two days.

Targets in the eastern Carolines were also hit from March, B-25s staging through Makin to fly missions against Ponape and Nauru. During two strikes on Ponape on 25-26 March, enemy fighters were encountered for the first time since January and one B-25 was lost, although eight were claimed by bomber gunners.

The 41st also took part in the final stages of the Marianas campaign when 11 aircraft of the 48th Squadron were detached to Saipan from 23 July to 21 August. Using their low level strafing technique with machine guns and 75mm cannon, the Mitchells flew 69 sorties against targets in Tinian and 91 against Guam, often accompanied by P-47s of the 318th FG. But by October with few worthwhile targets left in the Marshalls the 41st BG returned to Hawaii to collect new B-25Js and have some of its older Mitchells fitted with the J-type 8-gun nose, the 75mm cannon being dispensed with.

When the 41st returned to the war in June 1945, the long ranging groups of the 7th AF were joining up on Okinawa to become a unified force for the first time since entering combat. Installed at Kadena on 7 June, the 41st restarted operations on 1 July. On the 2nd, it was joined by the 319th Group, which brought the second

172
Eugene Olsen with his B-25C *Buzzin Beezee*, which was followed by *Beezee II* on a J model. *Eugene Olsen*

123

173
An ever-useful Cletrac being used as stand to get at the stabiliser damage to a 41st Group B-25C, with a G model jutting its nose in on the right hand side. Makin was not exactly over-burdened with workshop facilites.
USAF via NAA

twin engined type, the A-26 into the 7th's inventory.

The significance of Mitchells about to strike the Home Islands for the first time since April 1942 was not lost on one groundcrew man who reminded Maj N. V. Woods, preparing for the inaugural mission, that 'The last man to lead B-25s over Japan made lieutenant-general.' It had taken approximately 38 months of bitter fighting for the AAF to reach the point of repeating Doolittle's feat of arms.

Flying as a group, still something of a novelty for the hitherto far flung elements of the 41st, the B-25s struck Izumi airfield, Chiran, on 8 July. Proof that such missions still held dangers despite the enemy's position, was the loss of two aircraft during the airfield strike to Kyushu. Bombing and strafing attacks continued throughout the weeks prior to the surrender, the 41st also drawing enemy targets in China as well as Japan. The group also introduced a new weapon, the Mk 13 glide torpedo, to combat before the end. The two final missions came on 10 and 12 August, to marshalling yards at Tosu and Kanoya airfield, respectively. Crews reported low visibility and dust in the air — less than a week before the atomic bombs had been dropped on Hiroshima and Nagasaki.

Eugene Olsen flew 2,000 hours plus as a B-25 pilot, including two combat tours with the 41st. He was one of the first instructors to have a complete ground school training and pass through B-25 training establishments, at Greenville and Colum-

bus. Among other types, he also test flew the B-26 and A-20 as well as all combat models of the B-25.

As a captain flight leader in the 48th Squadron, Olsen often led not only the squadron but the entire 41st on occasions, and sums up the B-25 as: '... an honest military plane with no frills; I have looped and rolled them, splitessed them — they stay together! While the squadron was at Pearl, some of us would take our 25s up alone, or maybe with another pilot, just to get away from the boredom. We would buzz anything and everything. One thing I liked to do — and I never heard of anyone else nuts enough to do it — was to get up over Pearl and do a split S from 13,000ft — that was something! You had to do it just about right or all the coral dust would fill the plane and choke you when you rolled upside down just before the half loop down and pull out to level flight. You never forced the controls too much for fear the wings would come off.

'Then there were the two ways to make a fast landing: the first was a fighter-type approach, for which you always needed the control tower's approval. They never refused — but you made certain that you were not at a major airfield. You dove straight for the end of the runway in the direction you intended to land. At about 280mph and ten feet above the number painted on the end of the runway, you cut the throttles, hauled back on the column and turned left about 45 degrees into a hard pull-up turn. By the time you were up

174
Men of the 396th: These photographs of 41st Bomb Group crews were taken in early 1944, during the intensive series of operations to neutralise the Marshalls atolls of Julait, Maloelap, Wotje and Mille and Ponape and Nauru in the Carolines group. Thomas D. Thompson flew this B-25D (41-30825) to Tarawa from Fresno, California, via San Francisco, Hawaii, Christmas Island and Canton Island. *TNT* were appropriately, pilot Thompson's initials. Co-pilot was Bob Tappan. Photo dated 22 February 1944. *Thompson*

175
June Bug was Capt Edward Fiest's B-25D, shot down over Nauru on 11 June 1944. A Navy Dumbo PBY picked up the entire crew after three hours. Fiest had a broken back but recovered. *Thompson*

to about 400ft, you popped the gear out, started full flaps going down and opened the cowl flaps. You continued the roll all the way around back towards the end of the strip, all the time slowing down through 140-130-120 until just before going over the edge of the runway you were at about 85mph — and plip, you greased it in at 80!

'The other close-in fast landing was done by flying about 400ft over the end of the runway at about 200mph, cutting the engines, making a tight, level 180 turn downwind, dropping the gear, full flaps, cowl flaps and opening the bomb doors for extra drag. You then touched down right on the tip of the runway.

'Some of the enlisted crew members, if they had a really sharp pilot, would bet as much as $100 with other crews that "their" pilot could land a B-25 without spilling a drop of water! Only when they'd made the bet would they tell the pilot. Usually the answer the first time was, "Are you crazy?" After that it was something like, "I've told you dumb bastards before not to put me on the spot like this!"

'Usually, the procedure was to choose an ashpalt runway with numbers marked as the gamblers could add even money by insisting that their pilot could make a smooth as silk landing at the base of the number, or the middle or top, whichever they preferred. Then they took a GI canteen and its "cup", placed the cup on the centre of the pedestal just in front of the trigger switches and, just as the aircraft turned into the downwind leg, topped off the water to the very brim of the cup. (Needless to say, this had to be done in very calm air.) By the time you were on final, that cup was so full you had two enlisted men holding their breath (the pilot didn't breathe at all) because when those three tyres touched, even a slight jolt would spill the water. It was always nerve-wracking

and always ended with "Dammit, no more of this stuff — you're going to make me a guilty man one of these days."

'For a fast take off in the 25, we would roll on to the strip with the cowl flaps closed, push the throttles fully forward and drop full flap as we picked up speed. We could get off at about 85 mph by pulling the nose up as soon as we were off, raising the wheels and tilting the nose down. This let you pick up speed, as with the nose down you kept the plane right off the ground until you got to a safe flying speed. If one engine quit while you were doing this, they'd read about you in the newspapers . . . but with the flaps still fully down and about 100mph indicated, you could really get a B-25 up 300ft or so in a hurry. Incidentally B-25s were called "Zippers" in the 7th AF.

'When we went on a mission from Okinawa, we really had to have our heads out because each plane had to follow right behind another in a set order to be in the right place for take off. We would all start engines on a signal and then sit there, watching each plane go, looking for the serial number of the one we were to follow. This sounds simple enough — but if you had a hard time getting an engine started, it could cause all kinds of trepidation because you could screw up the whole mission!

'We used several ways to get airborne, one of which, providing the strip was wide enough, was two planes at a time, 20 seconds behind the preceding two, until everyone was off. Formations joined up in different ways: sometimes the leader would simply fly at reduced speed until everyone was in position and then gradually increase his power until they were all going at the same speed, rate of climb and so forth. Another method — and this was not tried until we got to Okinawa — was to take off one at a time at 20-second intervals. The first plane off would fly out for one minute, allowing 10

seconds for every additional plane behind him before making a 180-degress turn and come back at 500ft. The last plane would have that one minute and 20 seconds to get up to 500ft and make a sharp, climbing 180 turn to fit in behind the last plane. This system worked out pretty well, only because we were all very experienced by that time. Occasionally this technique was used by two aircraft at a time.

'Group missions were usually flown in stepped down formation, one squadron behind the other. Each squadron rotated as leader, number two etc, Sometimes the squadron CO would lead, but mostly a 1st Lt or captain flight leader would take it — or if his squadron was first on a mission, a 1st Lt or captain would actually be the group leader — we all took turns.

'Runways on Okie were either 100% coral, which was really great to land on or fly from, or steel mat. On these you had to be careful, as they sprang up and down. When landing, you were careful not to grease it in or you might find yourself back up in the air about to stall out — you flew it in hard so it would stay down.

'Okinawa was full of airfields and everything else! There were always about 2,000 ships of various sizes all around the island. Living conditions were always lousy; we slept in tents and hundreds of large rats continually ran through them at night. Maybe one man in 20 had an air mattress (if he cared to barter for one) but most of us slept on the canvas surface of the cot. We usually had one blanket and a mosquito net, never sheets though. There were also times when we slept in our cockpit seats.

'We usually flew our missions and lived in cotton flying suits and GI shoes; some of us mixed suntans and cut off the legs and arms as it was *hot* out there. We always flew with the pilot's side window open and in case of ditching carried a five-man and three-man raft. We always wore Mae Wests, too. None of us had one-man rafts until almost the end of the war, when our

176
A wingman photographed Thomas Thompson's B-25G-5 *El Bandido Borracho* during a mission to Ponape, late June 1944. The aircraft flew at least 38 missions. *Thompson*

177
Thompson's crew with a new co-pilot for *Bandido*, Lt Frank Pfyl, May 1944. *Thompson*

178
1-Lt Warren L. Eyer and crew with *Doc's Abortion II*. 'Doc' was Eyer's nickname. *Thompson*

CO made a deal by trading some washing machines or refrigerators someone had acquired from a B-29 outfit in the Marianas.

'We wore baseball caps or whatever else we could acquire and most pilots wore sunglasses, or goggles, occasionally. We all carried .45s and some kind of survival item in our knee pockets, like matches, a knife, candy or a tiny compass which would, along with a few other items, fit in a GI issue condom and be stuffed up your rectum if you were captured and not killed on the spot. The point to make here is that there were few B-25 prisoners — the

Japanese beheaded captured crews because the Doolittle raiders were the first enemies to ''invade'' Japan in 2,000 years — and they flew B-25s.

'Just before reaching a target we would don flak suits which fitted over our shoulders and if we could scrounge an extra one, we would stuff that down under our legs to protect our genitals. We would also put on those huge steel Navy gunner's helmets which would fit over our headsets. But boy, when we made a sharp turn or pull up, all that extra weight almost pushed you flat in your seat!

'Missions from Okie included a few to

177

178

China, especially the Shanghai area and Ching Wau airfield. For these mission we were issued with Chinese money in a sealed plastic bag, maps and directions on how to join up with Chennault's 14th Air Force if we had engine or other troubles. At any other time, like during our days in the Marshalls, we would have had engine trouble and flown to another air force — just to get out of the 7th!

'In any event, the B-25 flew all day on one engine, at 170mph. We usually flew at 185 indicated fully loaded for combat, at about 10-12,000ft, TAS approximately 210mph. When we went in on a target it was at full throttle — everything full forward. We didn't use ''military'' settings, just went right in and out as fast as we could — unless of course, a colonel or some other milk-run artist was leading. They would cruise in at 10,000ft and 180mph and we'd get our asses shot off! Of course, we were always briefed to go in at 8-10,000 and 180 but since it was our lives and ''they'' were not flying the missions, we would get a couple of thousand feet above our run-in altitude and dive down to pick up speed. Anything over 300mph was fairly safe — and don't fly in a straight line for more that 15 seconds!

'Jap guns could not track us at over 300mph, but had to lay a box of flak ahead of us. And it took about seven seconds for them to fuse, load and aim and another seven for the shell to get up to us.

'Mostly we carried four 500lb bombs with the top half of the bomb bay occupied by a rubber 215gal fuel tank. If you ever had any frag bomb hang ups — and we did — you stacked all the flak suits against the bulkhead and hoped and prayed that the plane would not blow up, even though the tank would be empty by then. There was no way to knock hung bombs out, as they usually caught on one end of a shackle. We flew with the bomb doors open when this happened; there was a small hole to look through after each bomb release and check that they'd all gone. If not, we would shake the plane and do everything possible to get the stuck bomb out. We came back from one raid carrying some of the 23lb bombs hanging. . .

'Other times we carried frag bombs, both singly and in clusters, to kill enemy gun crews, or incendiaries; all our bombs were armed before we took off because we could not get into the bomb bay once we were airborne. On our second tour we also had all our planes equipped to carry eight 5in rockets, four under each wing. You could fire two at a time, salvo all eight, or release them in sequence, two at a time. They were very accurate and really blew

things apart! You could blow up a house with two.

'Flight leaders would use a glass-nosed B-25J when the mission was at medium altitude, and wing ships dropped on the leader. Glass-nosed jobs were left behind on low-level missions, even though they had six forward-firing .50s for the pilot — we would simply take someone else's plane. The strafers gave us 12 fixed forward firing guns, plus the turret two — God what a noise those guns made! When they first fired, I about jumped out of my seat — I thought we had been hit!

'The pilot's control column wheel had various buttons for the guns and rockets; some were on the left side, including a double sided-button. The forward side was for charging the guns, with the index finger, the back, the side facing you, for firing the eight nose guns. On the right side was the button for the rockets and you also had a button for firing the forward side guns, which were manually charged by the bombardier/navigator or other crew member, depending on the B-25 model being flown. A high pressure air tank in the shape of a ball was used to charge the nose guns. Occasionally this ball would blow up and just scare the hell out of the pilot(s)! Some aircraft had a ''double'' button on the control wheel rigged to fire all the guns: the index finger for the four package guns

179
Taking it: Thompson and 2nd Lt Everett Lee Shirley, bombardier/navigator, examine the right wing flap of *TNT* punctured by a 20mm shell from a Zero that attacked on the 23 January Maloeap raid. Steel helmets and flak jackets were arbitrary (the latter for sitting on) and officers wore .45-cal automatics. Enlisted crewmen carried carbines and sub-machine guns. *Thompson*

and the left thumb for those in the nose. A button on the right side of the wheel charged the nose guns and at the end of the curve of the half-wheel was the mike button.

'There were not many problems with the B-25, although one thing that caused a few unnecessary deaths was the placement/rearrangement of toggle switches on the pedestal. One aircraft would have a bomb bay toggle switch on the pedestal, the next might have it on the left, yet another on the right — and some even had an actuating handle — always in different places.

'We received one replacement J model that had the carburettor air intake flap controls completely different from all the other planes. Our regular checklist (all mental, there was never a list written down) action was to pull back the two levers on the lower pedestal — or make certain they were well back, as that meant that the shut-off flaps were down and the engines would get the full quantity of air to the carbs. On this particular new model, which was given to 1-Lt Fred Deutsch, the lever had a neutral position! And worse, back was closed, exactly the opposite to what we were used to. Fred

had no trouble, but one day a new potential replacement pilot was given permission to take his father and some friends up for a ride from Machinist's airfield. This pilot's brother had been killed the week before in a B-17 crash and the young fellow apparently went through the pre-flight, flipped the handles back like he always did — but this time the flaps closed. He set up the engines and still didn't catch the mistake. The aircraft went roaring down the strip but never got off the ground. Off the end of the runway it went, across a gully and smashed through a bunch of tents on the other side. The plane exploded and burned, killed everyone inside. Not a single enlisted man in the tent area was injured. They were all at the mess hall waiting to go in — all except one who was stretched out on his back reading a newspaper and smoking a cigarette. The 25 came smashing through the tents and he was right in line. The tent was torn away and one wheel of the aircraft rolled across his belly and chest, knocking the paper out of his hands and the cigarette from his mouth. His belly and chest had diamond red marks from the tyre tread and the insides of each arm were red from where the sides of the tyre rubbed as it went by

180
Giving it out: There were plenty of targets for the 12-ship 396th Squadron attack, which came in over Maloeap at 11.20am line abreast, at zero altitude. At least seven Mitsubishi Zeros are visible, plus a twin-engined bomber. Thomas Thompson recalls that 35 Zeros followed the squadron 100 miles out over the sea, his B-25 being hit in the wing flap, having its turret and astrodome shot away and the radio mast lost under enemy fire. But by staying low the mediums survived and claimed two Zeros downed. One B-25 crash landed at Makin and all the others reached Tarawa. *Thompson*

181
Closer view of the approach to Maloeap airfield reveals one Zero destroyed in a revetment and camouflaged storage. The Zeros were painted black, Thompson recalls. *Thompson*

about 70mph! An absolutely unbelievable thing — unless you were there to actually see it. The guy was still petrified when Fred and I arrived and we were first on the scene.

'Our missions over Kyushu were really different — it was good to be flying over land, even though it was enemy held, instead of atolls and water, water, water! On 4 August about 80 of us went to Tarumizu on the west coast where they were apparently making parts for jet planes. We were to burn the town while B-24s bombed a factory. We carried four 500lb incendiary package bombs and each of the four squadrons of the 41st went in at low level. By the time we got there — the town was on the edge of a bay — we could actually see some of the bombs burning under the surf. We did our job and the whole place burned. One of the pilots supposedly dropped a couple of bombs that straddled our rescue submarine, surfaced in Kagoshima Bay, waiting for any of us who might have to land in the water. We saw him, but didn't believe the story, as no pilot should have had bombs left. In any case, it was startling to see our sub on the surface inside Japanese waters.

'Missions to Japan usually lasted about six hours and one raid that I led to bomb the Megazale railroad bridge with 82 planes was typical. It was cloudy — high cumulus up to 12,000ft — and we came up the east coast of Kyushu, made a left 180 degree turn to the bridge. Due to the clouds and 81 planes behind me, we ended up with a run of a minute and a half instead of 15 seconds — not too happy a situation. I laid my four 500 pounders diagonally right across the centre span and when the smoke and mud and garbage cleared it was still

there! And it was still there after the 81 other planes had dropped their loads. I heard rumours that it collapsed the next day with a train on it, but I just don't believe the Japanese were that dumb.

'As far as heroes go, the 7th Air Force had none unless, like in any air force, they were all heroes. Everyone did their job and wished they were somewhere else, in some other air force — like the 5th — or in China — anywhere in combat except with the 7th, where we were really wasted — until that is, we got to Okinawa and flew to Japan. Even then we were wasted at times. One outstanding milk run to Kyushu was led by the Group CO — 80 planes up from Okinawa to a cloud-covered Kyushu. We wandered around — lost — for what seemed like an hour. We were fired on by heavy AA guns on five occasions, never knowing where we were. Finally we were told to dump our bombs! We never even saw Japan and there was a lot of moaning and groaning over the radio like, "My God, where's he taking us now?" and "Does anyone know where we are?"

'Most of us had been out in the Pacific for more than a year and some of us were going into our twenty-first month or more. And there was the colonel, demanding radio silence. We just continued our smart-ass remarks because we knew that radio silence was not necessary. There were hundreds of bombers and fighters coming and going between Okinawa and Japan and besides, we needed the entertainment, a release from the continual possibilities of war. Because we wandered around for so long, some of the planes in the formation, mostly escorting Marine Corsairs, had to ditch on the way back, out of fuel.

'It was rare for us to lose aircraft in

combat at that time and although I don't recall how many B-25s went down on that mission, it was more than on any other raid out of Okinawa. A PBM picked up some crew members and finished up with 19 men aboard. I heard it had to taxi more than 200 miles to Ie Shima while the crew bailed out the split hull! We thought we had lost all those who went down to the sharks, as we had no word until the next day, when they were finally returned to us.'

Warren Lovell confesses to a life long love affair with the B-25, having flown it with the 7th from March 1944 until the end:
'I didn't get down to combat until July 1944, when the worst part was over and the Japanese fighter force was all but gone. The 41st was then on Makin and about to go to medium altitude attacks. My first two missions were to Juliat in the Marshalls at low level and were a little hairy. Whereas we couldn't estimate range very accurately (to use the 75mm cannon) the enemy gunners were both accurate and disciplined as we came in off the water. Naura was also tough in that while the number of guns was limited — I think only eight twin mounts, reputedly from Singapore, were there — they were very accurate. One squadron at a time would go up to Eniwetok and bomb Ponape and I went over for four missions.

'In October 1944 we went back to Wheeler Field, Oahu, and the old timers went home and I became a flight leader. We filled up with replacements and were in Hawaii until June 1944, which gave us an unusual chance to get very well trained.

While there, I tested a new sight for the 75mm, a weapon I really liked. The sight was like a Christmas tree and was an improvement in that we didn't have to adjust the sight for any change in range. It worked very well when we had the range worked out on the ground; we would start firing at about 5,000 yards and by the time the distance was down to 1,000 yards, we were quite accurate.

'I believe the manual called for three cannon shots a minute. The navigator, who loaded it, was supposed to reach up and tap the pilot's shoulder when the gun was ready to fire. But in combat, as soon as the pilot felt the breech block hit home, he knew he could fire. I know that with my crew we could get off 8-10 shots per minute. It was hot, sweaty work for the navigator — mine, Lt Warren Thornton, was very good but he did get a damaged kneecap from a recoiling cannon over Ponape.

'In the way of all things military, as soon as we were proficient with the cannon and sight, they changed them. We took out the cannon and put in the eight .50-cal machine guns. We thought we were going to the China coast initially, but at the end of June 1945 we left for Okinawa. It was a long route: Hawaii to Christmas Island on the first leg, then to Canton, then Tarawa, Eniwetok, Guam and finally Okinawa. Interestingly, the navigator in the five-man crew (B-25H model) I flew with had only trained in dead reckoning, but when we got to Hawaii our navigators received celestial navigation instruction and got very good at it. We would fly out, slightly to one side of the island we were going to and

182

182
Roaring out over the beach at Wotje on 7 Febraury 1944, Thompson's strike camera caught the shadow of a following B-25, exploding bombs and splashers from machine gun fire. Eight aircraft attacked during the eight hour mission from Tarawa, out and back. There was no fighter intercept, but heavy ground fire. No aircraft were lost. *Thompson*

183

183
Gun emplacements on Wotje caught by the strike camera, which usually took the B-25's tail bumper as well as the mayhem. One bomb is on its way here, during the 7 February strike. *Thompson*

then turn on a sun line. We thought nothing of a 1,000-mile single plane courier flight over water — we were young then...

'The 41st started bombing Japan from 1 July, but I was late getting to Okinawa and did not fly my first mission until the 16th. I then flew about every other day until the last mission on 12 August. The 7th Air Force had been essentially under the

Nimitz Navy command until we got to Okinawa (the 5th, 7th and 13th Air Forces became Far East Air Forces on 14 July, the 7th reverting from Navy to AAF jurisdiction) and we were the last AAF units to get there.

'For tactical bombing over Japan, we took over the island of Kyushu and the Kamikaze fields, particularly Kenoya on

185

185
Booty: A Japanese flag proudly displayed by Thomas Thompson and his crew on 7 March 1944, during the stopover on Kwajelein when the 96th moved from Engebi to Makin. *Thompson*

186
Back to Japan: Armourers prepare fragmentation bomb clusters for heartfelt delivery to the Japanese homeland by B-25 — for the first time since the Tokyo raid of April 1942. This was Okinawa on 30 June 1945. *USAF*

Kagoshima Bay in the south but I also hit Nagasaki, Sasebo and Kamanota. We would climb to about 10,000ft and bomb in a glide, utilising an attachment to the Norden bombsight that corrected for altitude. These attachments came from the Navy and as far as I know, we were the only ones using it. It was a great help as for one thing it gave altitude changes.

'There was some very heavy flak, particularly over Kanoya, which had over 70 guns. But all the good gunners must have been lost, for our losses were low. I flew about three low level attacks with rockets and napalm, one of which was to hit a railroad bridge on the east coast. At Kumamota we attacked railroad yards and then stayed on the deck to shoot at whatever we could find. Flying about 50ft off the deck and pulling up over power lines, we got heavy 20mm flak and I found that a quick burst at the towers would send huge balls of fire down the wires and stop the flak.

'We rarely saw fighters over Japan but always had our own top cover. At first the escort was Marine F4Us, then P-38s and P-51s. On 9 August I was just coming off the target over Kanoya when my radio operator, T/Sgt Charlie Hill, said over the intercom, ''Jesus Christ, look at that ... 3 o'clock!'' There was the mushroom cloud over Nagasaki ...

'It was quite an adventure, but I was glad when it was over. I didn't think they would surrender. My tail gunner had been killed on a low level as well as three out of the six of us classmates who had gone over together, but overall, our losses had been light.

'Among the interesting things that happened was the 47th Squadron training to use the glide torpedo. It was dropped at medium altitude, would shed its small wings and cruise in a set pattern once it was in the water. It was only used one or twice and I remember seeing one of them take a direct hit by pure chance over Nagasaki.

'The old Billy Mitchell was an awfully good aircraft; it took a lot of punishment and generally ditched well if necessary. After the war, I flew the B-25 again, in the California National Guard. In 1957 I went back into the Air Force as a major in the Medical Corps, still as a pilot and managed to fly a 25 one last time in the spring of 1958 before they were grounded.'

Flying Dutchmen

187
Survivors of the fighting in the
Dutch East Indies in 1942 who
had escaped to Australia
formed a number of Dutch
squadrons under RAAF
control. The first and only
Mitchell unit was No 18,
which formed on 4 April 1942
with a strength of five aircraft,
the rest having been
appropriated by the USAAF.
By June 18 more B-25s had
been delivered under Lend
Lease and eventually, at least
176 Mitchells were given
Dutch type letter-number
serial prefixes that identified
those machines operating in
the Pacific area. The
numbering system began in
the N5-120 range and these
machines, B-25C 41-12913
and B-25D 41-29723, which
crashed in the Darwin Sea on
18 February 1943, were early
examples. *via R. L. Ward*

188
Ex-factory B-25s bore Dutch
flag insignia and the last three
(or four) digits of the serial
number under the cockpit.
These machines, including a
B-25C-25, were photographed
at the flying school for Dutch
personnel established at
Jackson Field, Missouri in late
1943. Among the aircraft
assigned to the school were 20
Mitchells. Operational
machines were flown from
Jackson by new crews on
completion of their training.
NAA

189
Another early No 18 Squadron
aircraft was B-25D 41-29717/
N5-144 pictured here at
Canberra. It was ditched at
sea on an operational sortie on
18 February 1943.
G. J. Casius

190
For most of its wartime duty, No 18 occupied Batchelor airfield, Northwest Territory where this aircraft, B-25C 41-12936/N5-131 named *Pulk* was recorded on 4 May 1943. At that time, its pilot was Lt F. Pelder. *N. Geldhof*

191
Sgt Wynands of No 18 Squadron indicates his personal Donald Duck insignia on 41-12916, one of the longest serving Dutch B-25Cs. *N. Geldhof*

192
Heavy crash-landing for
Tangerine, B-25C-15
42-32483/N5-152 was the
result of an attempted night
take off from Batchelor on
22 May 1943. The lead
bombardier of the squadron,
Capt Jessurun, wound up with
the pencil he was using to log
the take off time stuck through
his throat when he was
thrown clear of the wreck.
N. Geldhof

193
In common with other
operators of early-model
B-25s, No 18 had a number
with field-modified tail
defence. *via R. L. Ward*

194
Fond Farewells: B-25D
43-3426/N5-192 *Palembang I*
provides the backdrop as
Dutch aircrew prepare to
leave Jackson, Missouri, for
Australia and the combat zone
in February 1944. The Dutch
flying school closed on the
15th of the month, the lack of
enough air and ground crews
preventing the formation of a
second Mitchell unit and
resultant transfer of a number
of Dutch aircraft to the RAAF.
N5-192 thus became A47-5.
Transfers of another kind
were made when many
American girls married
Dutchmen they had met at
Jackson. *G. J. Casius*

195
An armourer ramrodding the nose guns of 44-29030/N5-237 of No 18 Squadron in 1945.
Frank F. Smith

196
From front to back these NEI aircraft are: B-25D-25 42-87260/N5-188; B-25J-1 43-27692/'218 named *Grace*; B-25J-10 42-28184/'230 and B-25J-10 43-28182/'228. Many Mitchells that had seen WW2 service in Dutch hands faced further combat when the Japanese had been beaten. N5-228 was shot down by Indonesian flak on 4 August 1946 at Semarang, Java, during operations to qwell the uprising. *G. J. Casius*

197

198

197
Lack of armament suggests that this Dutch B-25J-25 (44-30505) is about to undertake a flight soon after the end of WW2. It became M-456 under the postwar designation system.
via Bruce Robertson

198
One of two B-25s which were painted with extra large Dutch flag insignia and flown over PoW and civilian internee camps in Indonesia on leaflet dropping sorties on 24 September 1944 and 28 January 1945. This aircraft is believed to have been N5-185. *G. J. Casius*

199
B-25D-25 42-87256/N5-172 was taken on RAAF charge on 10 February 1942 until 3 July 1945, when it was returned to Dutch service and used by the NEI pool squadron at Canberra. It later became M-372.

200
Unidentified B-25J of No 18 Squadron operating against the Indonesians subsequent to May 1947, when the Dutch national insignia was changed to a roundel and fin flash. Dutch aircraft flew bombing, recce and close support missions until 1949, when the Republic of Indonesia was established. *L. L. Peeters*

201
B-25J-15 44-28929, ex-N5-226 and J-25 (44-30505 ex-N5-256, now M-426 and '456 respectively, during the latter stages of the Indonesian fighting. Between sorties the ground crews stripped the Mitchells' camouflage paint back to bare metal — in most cases in preparation for the aircraft to be handed over to their former antagonists. Mitchells initially equippped No 1 Squadron of the Indonesian air force. *L. L. Peeters*

In at the Kill   Stanley Muniz

Flying as a radio operator-gunner with the 500th Bomb Squadron, Stanley Muniz joined the 'Air Apaches' in March 1945, by which time the 5th Air Force was gearing up for the invasion of Japan. The annihilation of Japanese bases outside the Home Islands was virtually complete and her naval forces and mercantile marine had been decimated. No longer did the US air forces in the Pacific want for adequate numbers of aircraft, equipment and personnel, a situation that brought some changes in operational procedures:

'By the time I joined the squadron, flight personnel were in a pool; we never flew as individual crews or had assigned aircraft. If the maintenance people could put ten planes on the line for a mission, any ten pilots, co-pilots, navigators, top turret engineer gunners and radio operator-gunners were selected. I don't think I flew with the same men more than once or twice. Everyone I spoke to wanted to fly as part of a crew and have his own plane like the crews in the 8th and 9th Air Forces, but we had more people than planes.

'This situation was highlighted after a rather rough mission by the 500th and 498th Squadrons on 4 April, a strike on Mako Harbour in the Pescadores, a small island chain off southwest Formosa. After it, we had only three serviceable aircraft in the squadron.

'Quite often we would borrow planes from other squadrons in the group and if we happened to lose one of them, we would have to replace it with our next new one flown up from the big depot at Biak — needless to say our squadron had more older planes than new ones . . .

'Because of the violent evasive action we always took in enemy-held areas, it was impossible for the radio operator-gunner to stand up, let alone aim and fire his guns at the waist positions. The result was that the waist guns were removed, the tail gunner taken off the crew and the radio man given the tail position. The ammunition that normally fed the waist guns was connected to the tail gun ammo cans and we were told not to be afraid to use it up. I also felt that the tail position was the "best seat in the house" especially so in my case as I almost always flew as lead radio operator and was able to see the rest of the squadron behind us doing their job.

'Some incidents that I recall include a shipping strike in the China Sea on Thursday, 29 March. We hit a convoy in fog and rain and my plane made runs on a "Sugar Charlie", a small coastal freighter with the super-structure aft like a tanker. We also made runs on a destroyer and a destroyer escort. The flak was quite heavy, but quite inaccurate due to the fog. We damaged the destroyer and freighter and were given credit for sinking the destroyer escort.

'On 4 August we made a maximum effort strike on Tarumizu on Kyushu. Mediums, heavies and fighters, almost everything that could fly in the entire 5th Air Force went along. There were airplanes all over the place and although the flak was very heavy, I didn't see any get hit. As my squadron approached the target from the land side — so we could make our getaway out over open water where there would be less flak, we passed over some high pointed hills. The Japanese had put flak guns on each hill and as my plane went over, we took a direct hit in the right wing. What saved us was the fact that we were so close to the gun that the shell went

202
Return to Clark: The 500th Bomb Squadron's corner of the main airfield in the Philippines, 1 June 1945.
USAF via Frank F. Smith

right through the wing and exploded above us.

'The flight behind saw what happened and one of the planes dived almost straight down and opened up with all 12 forward guns. That enemy emplacement just seemed to disintegrate. I had my old crew training co-pilot, Capt Seymour Nedic from Newark, New Jersey, to thank for that attack. He was then flying as a pilot and still rates my thanks — after all, we New Jersey boys stick together.

'As my plane left the target area, the whole coastline was in flames from one side to the other. The town was obliterated. It was like things I had read about in Europe, although I had never seen anything of that scale in the Pacific. We were told that Tarumizu held among other industrial targets, a rocket plane factory.

'When the war was over I remained in the Far East for a few weeks. After the articles of surrender had been signed, one of the two white-painted Bettys that had flown the Japanese emissaries to Ie Shima returned to Japan with documents from Gen MacArthur. I flew on the escort for that flight and had Capt Kenneth Waring of Miami as pilot. The Betty took off first, followed by the other escorting B-25 which took of in normal fashion. Capt Waring locked the brakes, brought the engines up to full power, and dropped the flaps. When he released the brakes, we shot forward like we had been fired from a catapault. As soon as he reached flying speed, Capt Waring hauled back on the controls and we climbed like a bouncing rubber ball — a real thrill for one of my last rides in a B-25.

'On 11 September 1945, I was on a two-plane flight that carried some civilians and army officers to Seoul, Korea. We left Ie Shima and flew to Kenoya, Kyushu, landed and refuelled on Japanese gas then flew to Seoul, where we were met by the Japanese who served cold beer.

'We remained until 14 September when we loaded up with leaflets, flew over an unknown town and scattered them. We then returned to Kenoya, refuelled and took off again for Ie Shima. The mission obviously had something to do with the peace arrangements for the Japanese in Korea, but we were never told the details.'

203
Reception committee: Japanese troops line the tarmac at Seoul, Korea, as one of two 500th BS B-25Js lands with personnel charged to assist the surrender arrangements, Tuesday, 11 September 1945.
Stanley Muniz

203

204
To the Victors the Spoils —
well a cool beer, anyway.
Japanese troops serve
refreshments to US aircrew at
Seoul. *Stanley Muniz*

Monument

205

205, 206
On 20 October 1943, Maj-Gen Jimmy Doolittle took the left-hand seat of a B-25D of the 12th Bomb Group during a visit to the 'Earthquakers', base at Gerbini, Sicily. Thirty-seven years later the most famous Mitchell exponent of them all again sat at the controls of a D model in the more peaceful surroundings of Castle Air Force Base, the three stars of his final military rank of Lieutenant General fittingly stencilled under the cockpit.
Howard Levy & NAA

206

As the most numerous American medium bomber to survive into the post war era, the B-25 enjoyed a long and useful life in the hands of military and civilian operators alike. It was not finally phased out of second line US Air Force inventory until the late 1950s and was to see many active years postwar service with a number of foreign air forces, including those of Indonesia, China, Peru and Venezuela.

It can perhaps be said that any aircraft still flying four decades after its first flight is the best possible tribute to its designers and manufacturers, and indeed the men whose exploits made it famous — there are still plenty of Mitchells around in the 1980s. While few of them actually fired their guns in anger in WW2, a good many have done so for the movie cameras, appearing in such productions as *Thirty Seconds over Tokyo, Catch 22* and *Hanover Street*. Others are prized museum exhibits, earmarked for less hectic retirement to commemmorate the deeds of that most terrible of all wars.

Early in 1980, North American Rockwell and the US Air Force honoured the man whose name is so closely associated with the B-25, Jimmy Doolittle. Then 83, the veteran stunt flyer, record holder, leader of the Tokyo Raiders and WW2 commander of three different air forces was invited to Castle AFB in Texas to be guest of honour at a unique ceremony. Its main purpose was to present a restored B-25 to the Air Force Museum at Dayton, Ohio, and recall the dark days of April 1942 when Doolittle's small force caught the imagination of the world. A highlight of the event came when the man himself climbed aboard the Mitchell and took the left-hand seat. Acknowledging the cheers of the 2,000 plus crowd, which included many former B-25 crew members, Doolittle gave a symbolic 'thumbs up'. Later he was quoted as saying that 'Even after all these years, the B-25 is a beautiful bird'.

The aircraft itself had been reconfigured by Rockwell as a gift to the musuem. Built as a B-25D-30-NA, serial number 43-3374 was subsequently modified to take three cameras in the 'toothache jaw' tri-metrogen nose fairing. After the war, it was placed in storage by MASDC at Davis Monthan AFB. Retrieved in 1957, by which time it was one of the few D models in existence in more or less original condition, it was extensively reworked to resemble the B model (40-2344) flown by Doolittle on the Tokyo raid. In the intervening years, the machine had acquired J-model waist windows and a rear observer's housing over the tailplane as well as the camera fit in the nose.

All non-standard items were removed and the aircraft sprayed in the authentic 1942 olive drab and neutral grey camouflage scheme, complete with red centre star insignia. So carefully was the work done that from some angles, it was hard to tell that you weren't looking at the genuine article. From the side and front, the give away was the separate exhausts rather than the single pipe type of the early model Mitchells.

207, 208
Nose and tail views of the B-25D-30 as modified for its post-war service and subsequently stored at Davis-Monthan AFB. *NAA*

207

208

209
Metamorphosis: Dedicated
labour turned the clock back
and 43-3374 became an
almost stock B-25B to
represent Doolittle's aircraft
(40-2344). The 'obsolete' USAF
serial was initially retained.
NAA

209